Arizona Highways
Heritage Cookbook

ARIZONA
HIGHWAYS BOOK

Text by
Louise DeWald

Color Photography: Richard Embry
Photographic Food Stylist: Pam Rhodes

Illustrations by
James R. Metcalf & Barbara Ritz

Measuring Up

A pint is a pound the world around, but what is a pinch?

A pinch	⅛ to ¼ teaspoon
A dash	¼ to ⅓ teaspoon
A few grains	less than ⅛ teaspoon
1 saltspoon	⅛ teaspoon
1 handful	3 tablespoons, level
1 wineglass	¼ cup
1 gill	½ cup
1 tumbler	1 cup
2 cups	1 pint
4 cups	1 quart
1 ounce butter	2 tablespoons
1 pound butter	2 cups
1 tablespoon cornstarch	2 tablespoons flour
1 tablespoon potato flour	2 tablespoons wheat flour

To taste: Now, that's up to the cook!

Oven Heat

Very slow	250 degrees
Slow or low	300 degrees
Moderately slow	325 degrees
Moderate	350 degrees
Hot	400 degrees
Very hot	450-500 degrees

About Ingredients

Unless recipes specify otherwise:

Flour is all-purpose, sifted before measuring.
Butter is salted butter.
Sour cream is the commercial type.
Eggs are large eggs.
Brown sugar is measured firmly packed.
Garlic cloves are medium.
Herbs and spices are fresh as possible.
Pepper is black pepper, best freshly ground.
Baking powder is double-acting.
All measures are standard and level.

(FRONT COVER) *A holiday feast comes from the oven in the Turner Ashby Hawes home which was built as a typical farmhouse of its era—the outset of World War I. Hawes, born in Virginia, moved with his family to Arizona as a young man, in 1887. Nettie Clay, later to be Ashby's bride, graduated from Tempe Normal School.*

Timbers for the house they built on the northeast corner of their Mesa farm came from an old Methodist Church in Tempe, which Hawes bought and demolished. The ground floor was adobe construction, and the upper floor wood framed.

Together, the couple raised five sons. After Ashby died in 1936, Nettie kept the farm going, then sold it to her third son, Wilfred, and his wife, Debbie. Two years after Wilfred's death in 1973, Debbie sold all but one acre—where the Hawes home now stands. After Debbie's death in 1980, the house was rented for a time, then stood vacant until it was sold in 1984.

The house has been completely restored and the beams from the old Tempe Church can still be seen in the concrete-enclosed cellar which supports the eighteen-inch-thick adobe walls. Mature trees screen the property and maintain its original peaceful, "country" feeling. The Hawes home is shown to visitors by appointment only.

(TITLE PAGE) *Legend says that Pipe Spring drew its name from a marksmanship feat by pioneer William (Gunlock Bill) Hamblin, who shot the bottom out of a pipe bowl without breaking the sides. Bill Hamblin visited the site in 1858 with his brother, famed Mormon missionary Jacob Hamblin. In the early 1860s, Dr. James Whitmore of St. George, Utah, obtained a land certificate for 160 acres surrounding the spring, and started a ranching operation.*

Whitmore's tenure as a rancher was rugged and brief. In January 1866, both he and his brother-in-law were killed, perhaps by Southern Paiutes, perhaps by Navajos who had eluded a roundup under the command of Kit Carson. The Utah Militia built a small rock fort at Pipe Spring, the beginning of the complex visitors see today at Pipe Spring National Monument. More grand than any other structure in the area, ranch headquarters became known as Winsor Castle, for Anson P. Winsor, operator of the ranch there for the Mormon Church.

The complex includes the orchard and garden, ponds, blacksmith shop, former militia barracks, bunkhouse used by explorer John Wesley Powell's survey crew in 1871, and other points of historic interest.

The volunteer taking bread from the oven is one of many who demonstrate pioneer skills for visitors.

Contents

Arizona Highways Heritage Cookbook

Hugh Harelson - Publisher / Wesley Holden - Managing Editor
Bob Dyer - Associate Editor / James R. Metcalf - Design and Production

Prepared by the Related Products Section of *Arizona Highways* magazine, a monthly publication of the Arizona Department of Transportation.

Printed in Japan.

Library of Congress Catalog Number 88-70338
ISBN 0-916179-16-8

Introduction

History, like an army, travels on its stomach. This Arizona heritage volume details the food of the territory from the tamales of Montezuma to the State House Stew of Prescott to almost anything grown and cooked before World War I.

Like Arizona's colorful canyons, Arizona cooking is carved from layers of the past. It begins with beans, corn, and chiles, and extends to other wild foods which named our towns: Ajo (garlic); Nogales (walnuts); Sonoita (place where corn will grow).

Here, then, is the stuff the state grew up on, recipes from an ever-changing Arizona.

Each recipe comes from a time when food was real, and most are vignettes of a person, a place, or a time in the state's incredibly varied story.

Indian recipes are included in each category: stews, breads, beans—cooked their ways—concluding with the natural bounty they did and do use. Their foods are so indigenous to Arizona's heritage that I made no attempt to put them into a separate category. Arizona's Indian tribes are scattered throughout the state, each preserving a strong sense of identity in food, dances, and customs. I cherish that.

The native American traditionally blessed what he ate, planted, or killed for food in the same spirit as 1 Corinthians 10:31 . . . *Whether therefore you eat or drink or whatever ye do, do all to the glory of God.*

Fray Pedro Font's Complete Diary of 1775-1776 said of the Yumans: "They are a gentle and happy people who farm the bottom land of the Colorado, growing wheat, maize, which they call Apache maize, orimuni beans, tepari beans, melons, and very large calabashas which they dry in strips."

His description of Mexican agriculture was complete. "They plant with a stick and grow maize, beans, squash, and chilis. With their fingers, they eat tortillas (unleavened bread) and beans, chilis, and tomatoes. The tortillas are corn, soaked in a weak lye, boiled until soft, then crushed at a metate. They begin their day hours before breakfast, stopping about 10 a.m. for maize cereal, sweet with honey or hot with red pepper. The main meal is in the early afternoon, usually tortillas, beans, and salsa. On special occasions, bits of meats in cornmeal are steamed in husks." Sound familiar, Mexican food fans?

The Spanish added cattle, swine, chickens, eggs, milk, citrus, and wheat to both the Mexican and Indian diets, a fair trade for the corn, potatoes, beans, cocoa, fruits, and turkey given to them.

Cochise Man developed primitive corn here 2000 years B.C. The Spanish were amazed also that our agricultural people stored rainwater, terraced, and used simple irrigation.

Anna Moore Shaw, Pima historian, recalled in her book, *A Pima Past*: "When Padre Kino came, he brought seeds of fig, pear, peach, quince, orange, pomegranate, mulberry,

---

The leading Navajo trader of his time, John Lorenzo Hubbell had an enduring influence on Navajo rugweaving and silversmithing. He demanded craftsmanship, and he knew how to promote it. He entertained Theodore Roosevelt at this made-to-order table.

Known as "Don Lorenzo" to whites, Hubbell was "Old Mexican" or "Double Glasses" to his Navajo friends. He was their merchant, trusted friend, interpreter of the white world, mediator with government officials, and an unselfish neighbor who opened his

home as an infirmary for victims of a smallpox epidemic.

Hubbell was born in New Mexico, the son of a soldier from Connecticut who married the daughter of an Hispanic family. To the Navajos, the Hubbell Trading Post was not only a place to get the goods they needed, but a social center as well—a place to meet friends, gossip, and learn the news from remote areas of the reservation. The trading post, now a National Historic Site administered by the National Park Service, has changed little since it served as a cultural crossroads in Navajo country.

onion, lettuce, cabbage, anise, pepper, and mustard. These took their places among the favorite foods of the Papago, Pima, and Maricopa. But the main little seed was wheat. It became an important part of the Indian economy. And during the time of the pioneers, it saved the life of many a white tenderfoot or soldier. Like the Nile, the Gila and Salt used to overflow their banks, depositing rich loam. The land belonged to everyone in the tribe. A man could clear as much as he could farm. Today our rich farms are very dry."

The Pimas sold wheat to the Mexicans of Sonora who used it, with typical ingenuity, to make flour tortillas, developing twelve-to-fourteen-inch circles, an impossibility with the traditional corn tortilla.

For desert dwellers, food, fiber, medicine, soap, and ceremonial potions came from cactus. Tender shoots of prickly pear or cholla were cooked in stew. The fruits were dried as sweets. Huge storage baskets were woven and filled for winter. Animal skin bags held jerky.

Primitive man used the animal stomach as a stewpot or a water bag, holding five to twenty gallons. The Navajos still relish the stomach for blood pudding, and the Apaches pit-bake cattle heads, as do many Mexican families today for holiday eating. Early trappers like Pauline Weaver and Bill Williams roasted an animal's heart, lungs, shredded fat, slivers of liver, and flesh in its stomach. Like a Son-of-a-Bitch Stew, it was considered delicious without seasoning.

The Hopis planted corn, squash, peaches, chiles, and pumpkins, and still do. The Navajos planted corn but preferred to herd sheep and goats, raiding many a Hopi garden (and still do). Pounded and dried meat and bean or acorn meal were the C rations of the Apache. If his horse gave out, he would cut its jugular vein and slice off a steak or two.

During the brief period when Arizona was under Mexican rule (1821-48), growth suffered because Apaches kept southern areas terrorized. Eventually, the strategic placement of forts and the enactment of legislation cooled warfare. The Apache Tribes were given twenty-seven percent of the Territory of Arizona.

The Spanish had encouraged frontier soldiers to bring with them their wives; the United States Army did the same. Some wives wrote little cookbooks about the elegant dining at camps such as Fort Huachucha. Others, like Martha Summerhayes, described the heat and lack of fresh food in Yuma as abominable.

Eating at the western portal of Camp Mohave was bitterly denounced in a soldier's journal: "Everything dries. Even chickens. There is no juice left in any living thing. Chickens hatched come out of the shell cooked. Bacon is eaten with a spoon and butter must stand in the sun an hour before the flies become dry enough for use."

The fixed menu served at Butterfield stations on the route of the Overland Stage (Apache Pass to Tucson to Fort Yuma) was dreadfully monotonous of necessity. Jerked beef, mesquite or pinto beans, corn cake, and black coffee, varied with antelope, venison, or mule meat, as luck had it. On a good day, apple pie smiled at the dusty diners.

A kind of census was taken in 1860, and the Arizona population was tagged at 6,482, including soldiers and tame Indians. For years, there had been petitions for separation from New Mexico. The Confederates took us in first. On February 24, 1863, President Abraham Lincoln signed a law creating the Territory of Arizona, just a few days more than a year after Jefferson Davis made Arizona a Confederate Valentine on February 14, 1862. We became a Union Valentine state only fifty years later.

The growth of the cattle industry took a healthy turn from 1866 to 1886, beef becoming the most important edible commodity, as Army posts and Indian reservations did less fighting and more eating. However, some historians believe sugar, coffee, and flour conquered more Indians than beef.

Hay in Phoenix, silver in Tombstone, copper in Jerome, and gold in Oatman meant boom camp luxuries. Fine hotels, restaurants, opera houses—then railroads and Fred Harvey—set a new standard in cuisine. For the cowboy in town, there were the lesser dining spots which hung out alluring signs: "Snack: two bits. Square meal: four bits. Bellyache: one dollar."

Chinese immigrants came to Arizona to help build railroads, and stayed on to help feed the growing populace. This cook worked at a Yuma-area mine about 1890.
ARIZONA HISTORICAL SOCIETY, YUMA

The Chinese who were brought in to help build railroads stayed to grow the greens which banished the threat of scurvy in the many forts and mining towns. At one point in Phoenix history, every downtown eatery had a full-house Chinese kitchen staff. But my Chinese friends told me their children quickly grew to prefer Mexican food over any other.

Out on the ranch, the chuck wagon cook, sourdough bread, calf fries, and beans were established as basics. Almost everybody did some gardening, and some butchering of pigs or cows, made butter, and canned, pickled, and dried.

In town or out, wood was chopped endlessly. "Many boys were doing a man's work at age seven and most women were married at sixteen," said Betty Accomazzo, who has compiled and written nine volumes of *Ranch Histories* about families who homesteaded here. "We are fortunate that we can get first-hand accounts of what ranch life was actually like eighty or ninety years ago from the people who lived it." And firsthand recipes of unforgettable foods corralled

for this book: Lumpy Dick, Vinegar Rolls, Mesquite Bean Bread, Sourdough Biscuits, and hundreds more.

Heritage food is Dutch oven cooking, pit roasting, Mormon baking, fresh fish fries, lambecues, and Cornish pasties. It's Camp Meeting Buttermilk Pie, Acorn Stew, and Bisbee Lady Baltimore Cake.

The author has visited every possible kitchen, campfire cookout, fiesta, fair, rodeo, contest, tent, river, and patio food happening in the past twenty-four years. For those who remember how it was and for those who want to know, here are recipes from handwritten scrapbooks, cupboards and trunks, old church cookbooks, and grammy's memories.

Whenever possible, a snatch of reminiscence credits each recipe for a cooking memory given as freely and cheerfully as food left on the back of the stove by our pioneers who practiced Latchstring-Is-Always-Out hospitality.

— *Louise DeWald*

Chapter 1
Openers and Closers

Appetizers once were celery and carrots iced in Grandma's cut-glass dish. Soup began the meal. Slowly but surely, the appetizer rose to tempting importance, the soup course waned, and imbibing increased.

Favorite appetizers appeared and held on, mostly the quickly-popular dips. Bean and guacamole dips, fresh salsa or cheese melted with salsa ingredients, and some form of meat with sauce—meat balls or steak chunks or strips. They are more than delectable; they're useful.

Marguerite Noble, Payson novelist and historian, said it best: "A sturdy dish of hot beef appetizers does much to steady the company, keeping the guests upright."

Eye-openers used to be fairly simple except for the mule-kick margarita. Older thirst quenchers began with fermented cactus beverages considered sacred by many Indian tribes. Nutritious corn atoles and foaming versions of chocolate were gifts of Mexico.

In this state's heritage, the most used eye-opener of all has been that black stimulator brewed from the noble coffee bean. Arbuckle's, dark roasted in sugar, was the favorite brand. Ramon F. Adams, noted historian, wrote: "The cowman likes his coffee black as a stovepipe, thick enough to plow, and strong enough to float a horseshoe." He credited Arbuckle coffee with winning the West.

The ladies tamed it into a gentler brew, duding it up on special occasions with whipped cream and assorted brandies.

Not Mormon ladies, however. They remained faithful to wheat drinks, as do their families.

It is interesting to speculate on why brothers Timothy and Michael Riordan chose to build a monumental duplex as their family homes. The brothers were utterly dissimilar in interest and tastes. Timothy was a big, bluff, hearty outdoorsman; Michael tended to be frail and rather scholarly. Tim had been a merchant in the Chicago area before seeking his fortune in Flagstaff. Mike had entered the Jesuit novitiate, but two bouts with tuberculosis sent him to Arizona. The brothers married two sisters, Caroline and Elizabeth Metz, who were cousins of the Babbitts, another family that made indelible marks on the economic and political life of Northern Arizona. So the stage was set for construction of Kinlichi Knoll.

A new building fad, the American Craftsman movement, was hitting full stride when the Riordans began construction of their estate. Its rustic design was stylistic rebellion against Victorian ornamentation, and suited a pair of frontier lumber barons. Rather than one mansion, Kinlichi Knoll is two mansions—built at a forty-five-degree angle and connected by a thousand-square-foot ballroom and billiard room. Similar in style and design, the two homes nevertheless reflect the different tastes of their occupants.

One of the most striking features of the first-floor family rooms is the tulip-motif, Tiffany stained-glass windows, a total of thirty-one panels. Interestingly, when built in 1904, Kinlichi Knoll had two telephones—exactly one-half of Flagstaff's telephone system.

The ballroom, pictured, was where Timothy Riordan retreated for his after-dinner brandy and a hand-rolled Havana cigar.

Cowboy's Delight

Doris Seibold, ranchwoman of Patagonia, collected the folklore of Southern Arizona so well, she earned herself a niche in the National Cowgirl Hall of Fame and Western Heritage Center.

Her appetizers are steak strips and little hot biscuits, heritage from the late 1800s, when 12,000 cattle ran the Patagonia range.

Use skirt steaks or use the small ends of filet mignons. For a crowd, use the entire filet, also called backstraps. Town cooks can ask the butcher for skirt steak or tenderloin. Cut slices 2 inches long by ⅜ inch thick. Flatten to ¼ inch with wooden mallet or edge of a plate.

For indoor cooking, use a Dutch oven or big, deep iron skillet. Combine flour, salt, and pepper. Dredge meat lightly in flour mixture. Heat oil to sizzling hot and fry meat strips quickly, 2 to 3 minutes for rare, no more than 5 minutes, ever.

For outdoor cooking, sink Dutch oven into a bed of coals ½ hour before using. Proceed as above to cook. Or use pointed sticks over a campfire and let each cook his own.

For the grill or hibachi, grill 2 to 3 minutes above the coals. Pieces cook very quickly.

In all cases, serve at once with hot biscuits.

Dropping meat in a skillet of braised chiles, spices, and onions transforms the strips into fajitas.

2 pounds tender beef steak
¼ cup flour
1 teaspoon salt
¼ teaspoon pepper
¼ cup cooking oil

Guacamole

Guacamole transformed the humpy, dark avocado into the Mexican Cinderella of dips. Always use lime juice, not lemon.

Halve avocados, remove pits, saving one. With spoon, remove meat from shells and mash coarsely in bowl. Add remaining ingredients, except Tabasco. Turn into serving dish, add reserved avocado pit to keep Guacamole from turning dark (it works), and cover tightly. Refrigerate. Never make up more than 2 hours before serving. Remove pit to serve and surround with warm, salty tortilla chips. Serves 4 to 6.

2 large, very ripe California avocados
¼ teaspoon salt
2 tablespoons finely chopped fresh cilantro
2 green onions, finely chopped with a few tops
½ teaspoon fresh lime juice
¼ teaspoon pressed garlic juice
Tabasco sauce, optional

Refried Bean Dip

Refried Beans, or Frijoles Refritos, are Mexican by birthright and traditionally were mashed with a little bacon drippings.

Heat bacon drippings or oil in heavy cast iron pot or pan over low heat. Add cooked beans and stir, so all beans are coated. Add enough liquid that beans can be mashed, using wooden spoon. Some like beans very smooth; others prefer them lumpy. Add cheese, either way, using Monterey cheese if goat cheese is not available. Beans are best done ahead of time, then reheated with a little more bacon fat, to be served hot with tortilla chips.

A zestier dip may be offered when ½ cup chopped green chiles and 1 clove chopped garlic are added to beans. For flame eaters, add a teaspoon or more of chopped jalapeños.

6 cups cooked pinto beans
1 to 2 cups bean cooking liquid
¼ cup bacon drippings or corn oil
1 pound grated goat's milk cheese

Lobster con Queso

Among the rugged crags of the red canyon walls of Sedona once stood Oak Creek Lodge, famous for two generations of cooks. The Mayhew family opened the lodge when the road was a wagon trail. A Mayhew daughter, Mrs. Al Wohlschlegel, cooking on the original giant wood stove, added lobster to traditional chile con queso. The luxury of lobster, the zip of salsa, and the creamy binding of longhorn cheese made this dish memorable.

Sauté onion and bell pepper in hot oil. When onions are transparent, add salsa, and simmer. Dice or chop tomatoes to add to sauce. Cook until tender, adding chili powder. Taste. Add salt and pepper, if necessary. Gently stir in lobster. (Use 1 cup canned lobster if fresh is not available.)

Add grated cheese and the cream. Heat until very hot, stirring with wooden spoon. Transfer to chafing dish and have ready small plates and large chunks of fresh, crusty bread. Guests dip and serve themselves, fondue style. Enough for 8 as an appetizer.

¼ cup chopped green onions with tops
½ bell pepper, finely diced
1 cup green chile salsa
3 cups canned tomatoes, with juice
2 tablespoons corn or olive oil
1 teaspoon chili powder
1 cup lobster, cooked and chunked
1 cup grated longhorn cheese
½ cup heavy cream
loaf crusty fresh bread

The boat-shaped dining table matched the shape of the Timothy Riordans' dining room in their wing of Kinlichi Knoll, impressive duplex mansion built in Flagstaff by the Riordan Brothers, lumber barons and civic leaders. The home, probably the largest private dwelling in Northern Arizona, now is a State Historic Park.
ARIZONA STATE PARKS

Remembering the Good Old Days

"The first so-called Arizona Pioneers' Reunion was in 1921 under the sponsorship of Dwight B. Heard, then owner of *The Arizona Republican*. Nearly 3,000 attended at Riverside Park. Many feel they are living in a new world and wish there were still things of the old days.

"Just thinking about grinding up the coffee kernels in an old home-size hand mill, or of roasting the green berries in the oven gives them a feeling of nostalgia.

" 'My, but those old Arbuckle sugar-glazed coffee beans, put up in pound packages for ten cents, sure beat anything you can buy today. Everything nowadays is in too fancy packages. There's just no end to the labor saving devices you have to buy in these times,' were remarks often heard."

Roscoe G. Willson in
Arizona Days and Ways Magazine
April 6, 1958

Calf Sale Coffee

During the depressed '30s, Arizona cattlemen banded together to finance beef promotion. Roy Hays offered his Yavapai County ranch for a calf sale every September, with pit barbecue and drums of coffee. Wives added groaning tables of cakes and pies. Everyone ate too much but, due to the quality of the coffee, nobody fell asleep. The sale and the coffee remain the same—an event and a drink you have to admire.

water
30-gallon container
2½ pounds coffee

To make about 240 cups of respectable coffee, bring water to a boil, shy a gallon, in a 30-gallon container. They use a big oil drum, more than reasonably clean, over coals. Drop into the rolling water a muslin bag filled with 2½ pounds fresh coffee. Reduce heat and place a sterile, green mesquite stick across the top of the drum. This is the best way to keep coffee from boiling over, IF heat is reduced soon enough. A few foam-flecked grains usually escape into the brew, and a light foam may spread across the surface until the coffee reaches the gently bubbling stage. By then, it is rich and strong. Throw in a pint of cold water. That settles it into perfect Western coffee, ready for dipping out.

The question comes: How do you like your poison? The answer: Barefooted. No canned cow for me.

The Arbuckle Thumps

At one point in coffee history, the Arbuckle Brothers of Pennsylvania had the cowman's business tied up with a bean which became a classic. Until after the Civil War, beans were packed green. The Arbuckles began specializing in coffee beans roasted with sugar and egg white to seal in fresh flavor. They packed it in bags with a picture of a flying angel, a streaming red banner at her throat (a Red Baron in reverse).

Brilliant merchandisers, the Arbuckle boys packed coupons worth saving for razors or alarm clocks and bagged sticks of peppermint candy in each coffee sack. Anyone who ground a pound had first crack at the prize. Yet it was the strength and flavor of Arbuckle coffee that made it so popular it was commonly ordered by the case, especially at the ranch. Black and rich and hot, coffee was a necessity at every meal as well as before and after riding or guarding the herd, day or night.

Coffee soup: Bread or biscuits with canned milk, syrup, and coffee made a hot and stimulating breakfast for a generation when time or the larder did not permit eggs, potatoes, and sausage. Dessert was often one more biscuit with lick (molasses) and a final cup of coffee.

The Arbuckle Thumps are the accelerated, thumping heartbeat that comes with intake of too much strong coffee, admiringly credited to Arbuckle, the coffee that kept the West awake, oldtimers said.

Placida's Atole
(Champurado)

Placida Smith, friend of the foreign born, for many years was the spirit of Friendly House in Phoenix, where aliens came to learn citizenship and train for work. She told me about Atoles, used in Mexico for invalids, for nursing mothers, and after fevers. "But they are also a most delicious breakfast drink, a meal in a cup."

Toast corn kernels until brown. Grind even finer than cornmeal. Stir the brown sugar and the cinnamon into the ground corn, mixing well. Into the 2 cups boiling water, stir 1 cup of the corn mixture, cooking over low heat 5 minutes, stirring the while. Remove from heat. Into each serving cup, place enough of the mixture to fill halfway, then add hot milk, and stir or whip to froth. Refrigerate unused mixture. Recipe makes about a dozen cups of Champurado.

1 cup brown sugar
1 pound dried corn kernels
1 teaspoon ground cinnamon
2 cups boiling water
hot milk

Outpost Coffee

The Mormon version of Atole became known as Outpost Coffee. They preferred grinding wheat, rather than corn, to make a nutritious drink—minus the Arbuckle thumps. Wheat, and sometimes cornmeal, was mixed with an egg and some sorghum molasses, then toasted on a pan in the oven. Like instant coffee, they blended it with hot water and milk.

Edens Eggnog

Thomas L. Edens Sr. was architect, contractor, and builder of the Hotel Westward Ho, the Arizona State Fair grandstand, and the Carnegie Library, all in Phoenix. His daughter, Delia Edens Dorsch, recalled at age 80 that when Phoenix had a rare hailstorm, he came home quickly, gathered hailstones, and made her vanilla ice cream. On other special occasions, he was noted for this powerhouse eggnog.

Beat egg yolks with sugar until very light. Stir in milk, whiskey, and rum with a little nutmeg. Fold in cream and egg whites, beaten until stiff. Serve very cold, with a drift of freshly grated nutmeg on each cup. Makes 4 quarts.

12 eggs, separated
1 cup sugar
1 quart milk
nutmeg to taste
2 cups whiskey
1 cup rum
1 quart heavy cream, beaten

Margarita

Tequila, Mexico's national liquor, is a blend of Indian and Spanish civilization. Legend says a lightning bolt blasted the maguey plant and when Indians tasted the fiery, burnt juices, that species of the agave family became an object of worship.

The Indians fermented the agave juice, nothing more. The Spaniards distilled it.

The classic way to drink tequila is taking it "neat" with a lick of fresh lime and rough salt. From that evolved the Margarita, which Arizonans have made their unofficial state drink.

Drop ice cubes into blender; whirl once. Add tequila, Cointreau or Triple Sec (orange liqueur), and fresh lime juice. Whirl just to slush. Rub squeezed lime around rim of stemmed glass. Turn rim in saucer of salt to coat edge. Fill glass and sip Margarita through frosted rim. Margaritas are best icy cold.

2 jiggers tequila
1 jigger Cointreau or Triple Sec
juice of ½ fresh lime
1 saucer of salt
3 cubes ice, crushed

Elderberry Cordial

Big Jim Hennessey, cow and sheep man of Flagstaff and Peoria, shared these two libations from a time when after-dinner drinks were made at home.

Gather enough ripe elderberries to make a pint of juice. Add a pint of good, fresh molasses. Boil, stirring constantly, for 20 to 25 minutes. Remove from heat. When cool, add 1 pint of brandy, stirring to blend. Have ready 3 crystal or cut-glass decanters, freshly rinsed with hot water. Fill with cordial and stopper securely. Store in a cool, dark closet. Can be used after a month, but keeps indefinitely. Also good for a bad cough.

1 pint elderberry juice
1 pint molasses
1 pint brandy

Blackberry Cordial

Crush 2 quarts fresh blackberries in a deep saucepan. Cook in their own juice, stirring often. When berries are soft, strain the juice and measure it into another pan. For each cup of juice add 2 cups sugar. Boil until sugar is dissolved, then take off heat to cool. Add brandy equal to the amount of juice. Mix well and strain into sterilized jars. Seal with paraffin and allow to stand at least a month before serving. Sip and savour with deliberation. Warms you like a small fire.

2 quarts blackberries
sugar
brandy

Chapter 2
Stews and Soups:
The True Potluck

The first stewpot in Arizona undoubtedly was an animal stomach. Indians and pioneers brought home not only the meat but the pot, which became a liquid-proof vessel for stew or soup. It also made a sturdy water bag, some holding from five to twenty gallons. The Apache, Navajo, and Yaqui Indians still use the stomach—primarily for cooking blood pudding.

Classic stews of the West include the fiery menudo (sure cure for a hangover) and the cowboy stew known affectionately as a son-of-a-bitch. Basic ingredients for both come, again, from the inside of an animal.

Soup is more liquid and more civilized than stew. Cookbooks of the early 1900s began soup chapters with an earnest discussion of stock. "A crock of well made stock is indispensable for every well ordered household," exhorted *The Table Cookbook.*

Everybody had some kind of garden. Soup was the natural gathering place for vegetables, bones, herbs, and suet. Almost everyone had a few chickens, the old and tough ever kettle-bound. Medical science has agreed, finally, with mama that chicken soup is good medicine.

In the food-stew history of Arizona, there are none lauded as "gourmet." Soup, on the other pot, assumes many roles—elegant, hearty, thin, thick, ethnic, and basic.

Established as a temporary army camp in 1877, Fort Huachuca owes its birth to the Indian fighting of the '70s and '80s. Its role was to protect settlers in the southern part of the Arizona Territory, safeguard travel routes in the area, and prevent Apaches from using their traditional escape routes into Mexico.

The fort's site was selected for its fresh water supply, abundance of trees, high ground, and good observation in several directions. Designated a fort in 1882, it was named a few years later as the advance headquarters for General Nelson A. Miles' campaign against Geronimo. When the Apache threat waned, Fort Huachuca remained on the Army's active list because of continuing border raids by bandits, renegades, and outlaws. Before World War I, the "Buffalo Soldiers" of the 10th Cavalry arrived for a twenty-year stay that included service across the Mexican border under General John J. Pershing.

Subsequently, the post was home of the 93rd and

92nd Infantry Divisions, training for their combat roles in World War II.

Today's Fort Huachuca is a high-tech center serving as headquarters for the U.S. Army Information Systems Command, the Army Intelligence Center, and as the Army Electronic Proving Ground. The Fort's Historical Museum, which is open to the public, portrays not only the story of Fort Huachuca itself, but the colorful history of the U.S. Army in the American Southwest.

B Troop, 4th Regiment, U.S. Cavalry (Memorial), now projects the color and excitement of a uniformed frontier cavalry unit through special appearances all over the Southwest. Mounted on traditional McClellan saddles, armed with sabers and carbines, and wearing Army blue and cavalry yellow, the troop commemorates a unit that actually served at Fort Huachuca in the 1880s. L Battery, also appropriately outfitted and armed for the era, provides artillery support.

1890 State House Stew

Lester Ward (Budge) Ruffner, Prescott historian and author, traces State House Stew back to the days when his Uncle George Ruffner was sheriff of early Yavapai County. Anytime the sheriff's friend, Arizona Governor B. B. Moeur, came to dinner he always requested—and got—this beef-and-biscuit dish.

Bring beef to a boil in water to cover in heavy pot. Remove any resulting scum, then season to taste with salt, pepper, oregano, sweet basil, and bay leaf. Cover and simmer until tender. Remove meat and bay leaf. Set beef aside. Season flour with salt, pepper, and paprika to taste. Add vegetables to broth and cook. Roll drained meat in seasoned flour. Brown on all sides in small amount of hot shortening. This is the secret to State House Stew's popularity: browned, seasoned, tender meat with juicy vegetables. Strain broth through several layers of cheesecloth. Place meat on platter and vegetables in bowl with juice. Serve with hot biscuits, well coated with melted butter before baking to ensure golden crust firm enough to sop up juices without sogging. Secret number two: those butter-crunchy biscuits.

2 pounds fresh beef stew meat, cut in chunks
water
salt and pepper
oregano, sweet basil, and bay leaf
shortening or oil
¼ cup flour
paprika
6 to 8 carrots
2 onions, quartered
6 potatoes, peeled and quartered

Son-of-a-Bitch Stew

Cowboy stew is also known as Son-of-a-Gun, Forest Ranger, Supervisor, Mother-in-Law, Boss Man, and, most colorfully and commonly, as Son-of-a-Bitch. Even the mother-in-law of the late Arizona Governor George W. P. Hunt used that name when she made her stew on the old QS Ranch in Pleasant Valley. This cowboy stew is an all-out version I tasted at the OU Ranch in Skull Valley when I was helping doctor calves at roundup. Marguerite Hazlewood bossed it.

Cut everything into little pieces, keeping the brains separate. Cover all except the brains with water and boil at a slow roll about 4 hours. Have brains freshly washed in cold water, then add to stew, and cook another half-hour. Add more water and salt as needed. Watch closely after brains are added; stew scorches easily. Never add spices or vegetables to a Son-of-a-Bitch; spoils the true flavor of the ingredients. This amount serves about 14.

all the marrow gut from a freshly butchered calf
all the brains
all the butcher's steak (strips of meat hanging from the ribs)
all the sweetbreads
½ of the heart
1 piece of liver the size of your hand

Sheepherder Stew

The sheepherder, like the cowboy, often relied on a chunk of meat that did not spoil and could survive weather changes. Jerky and salt pork filled the bill and the stomach. Isolated cooks, like Mrs. L. D. Harbison of Phantom Ranch at the bottom of the Grand Canyon, needed this recipe, too—her standby.

Slice salt pork into skillet, enough to cover bottom. Add a layer of sliced onions, then a layer of sliced potatoes. Alternate until the skillet is full, sprinkling with red or black pepper, or both. Cover with water. Place over low heat, covered securely so stew will steam. Cook slowly ½ hour, or until potatoes are tender. Sourdough bread and stewed tomatoes are good buddies with this stew. Serves 6.

1 pound salt pork
3 large onions
6 large potatoes, peeled and sliced
pepper, black or red
water

Cocido

Cocido is an important Mexican family dish similar to the French pot au feu, in which soup broth, meat, and vegetables are meant to last for several meals, always better with time.

Cut meat in cubes. Peel onions and wash well other vegetables and fruits, but do not peel. Start with the meat, bacon, garbanzo beans (chickpeas), potatoes, cabbage, and turnip, placed in a large pot in water to cover. Cook a half-hour. Remove any scum, add the cumin and other vegetables. Cook over low heat until everything is tender. Add fruit, whole, and cook gently until fruit is tender, adding salt and oregano the last half-hour. The soup broth may be served first, then the meat and vegetables, with a hot sauce if desired. Finally, serve the fruits, sliced.

1 pound fresh pork
2 pounds stew beef
3 slices bacon
1 cup cooked garbanzo beans
2 white potatoes
2 sweet potatoes
½ head cabbage
1 turnip
1 pinch cumin
1 bunch carrots
1 stalk celery
2 onions
1 apple
1 pear
2 summer squash
1 teaspoon salt
1 generous pinch oregano

Mutton or Lamb Stew

The Indian cowboy did not share the feelings of the Anglo cowman, who was profanely derisive of eating mutton or lamb. To the Hopi and the Navajo, sheep meant good weaving and good eating.

Wipe meat with damp cloth and trim off fat. Brown a little fresh, white fat (not old, yellow fat) in heavy pot. Brown the onions in the fat until golden. Add the lamb or mutton and brown well on all sides. Peel blackened portions from roasted chiles. Unless stew is wanted throat-puckering hot, remove seeds and inside fibers from chiles. Chop and add to stew. Red potatoes can simply be scrubbed and quartered, but if old white potatoes are used, peel and dice. Add to pot, cover all with water, and bring to a rousing boil. Reduce heat, cover stew, and simmer 1 hour. Add wild onion, salt, and pepper. Simmer another hour, covered. Best eaten with sturdy Hopi oven bread. Serves 6 to 8.

3 pounds mutton or lamb stew meat, or riblets
3 or 4 green chiles, roasted
2 big onions, diced
6 potatoes, small red preferred
wild onion, when available, sliced
salt and pepper to taste
1½ quarts water

Some officers' wives were able to see that their frontier-soldiering husbands had comforts to come home to, as evidenced by this Victorian parlor in officers quarters at Fort Huachuca, photographed in 1894.
FORT HUACHUCA MUSEUM

Sopa de Albondigas

Chop beefsteak very fine and mix with cornmeal. (This was before hamburger.) Rub into chopping bowl a spoon of lard. Add chopped meat mixture and break in the egg. Season with salt and pepper. Cut up the onion, garlic, and tomato. In a large pot, over medium heat, melt meat drippings. Add vegetables and simmer while mixing rice with spices and meat. Knead this mixture 5 minutes. Roll into balls the size of a walnut and drop one by one into vegetables. Add boiling water. Simmer 1 hour. Serves 4. An early-1900s Tucson cookbook provided this recipe from the Fred Ronstadt family.

1 pound beefsteak
½ cup cornmeal
1 large spoon of lard
1 egg
salt and pepper to taste
1 onion, cut fine
1 clove garlic, diced
3 tomatoes, chopped
2 tablespoons meat drippings or lard
1 tablespoon raw white rice
3 fresh coriander leaves, chopped
3 peppermint leaves, chopped fine
1 teaspoon dry seeds of parsley
½ teaspoon wild marjoram
1 quart boiling water

Pumpkin Soup

Early settlers along the Salt River grew hay and barley as money crops, watered by irrigation after 1867. Pumpkins took over so many patches, pioneers named the area Pumpkinville. Silver-tongued Darrel Duppa persuaded them that Phoenix was a more poetic and fitting name. Pumpkin Soup remained the same.

Cut pumpkin into chunks and remove seeds and fiber. Pare off any bumpy outer skin. Cook pumpkin chunks in boiling, salted water to cover, until tender. Drain and put through sieve or colander. In soup kettle, combine 2 cups of pumpkin puree with the butter, brown sugar, and seasonings. Stir with a wooden spoon a few minutes, cooking over low heat to mingle flavors. Stir in hot milk, one cup at a time. When well blended, stir gently to heat through. Serve with toasted bread cubes. If too bland, a drop of hot pepper sauce (Tabasco) will add zip. Serves 4.

½ small pumpkin
2 quarts boiling, salted water
3 tablespoons butter
1 tablespoon brown sugar
1 teaspoon salt
¼ teaspoon white pepper
3 cups hot milk
hot pepper sauce, optional

Chicken Gumbo Soup

Meals were 25 cents and upward, according to the 1886 Russ House menu in Tombstone. Miss Nellie Cashman, manager, chose Chicken Gumbo Soup for Thanksgiving dinner that year, complete with the oysters she bought by the barrel.

Place cut-up chicken in 6-quart Dutch oven. Add water and half the salt and bring to a boil. Reduce heat, cover, and simmer until chicken is tender, 2 hours. Cool enough to remove chicken and strip meat from bones; cube. Skim fat from broth. Add chicken, okra, onion, tomatoes, thyme, and red pepper. Stir lightly, add remaining salt, and cook 15 minutes, covered. Add oysters and cook until edges of oysters curl; no more than another 10 minutes. Serves 10 to 12 in cups, as soup. Or serve over boiled rice in bowls, as gumbo.

4-pound stewing hen, cut up
7 cups water
1½ teaspoons salt
1 pound fresh okra, sliced
½ cup chopped onion
28 ounces tomatoes, with juice
1 sprig thyme
¼ pod red pepper
1 dozen oysters in juice

Depression Soup

Margaret Shellabarger Axtell and her husband, Dwight, survived ranching through the days when cattle starved or were slaughtered by the government, pigs got cholera, and drought or grasshoppers devastated crops. Soup was the answer to hunger. More than one meal was coaxed out of a turkey carcass or a ham bone, even the water in which they cooked. Margaret chuckled with sympathy at a bachelor neighbor's complaint: "I had a friend I got on with until I loaned him my soup bone. He went and cooked black-eyed peas with it and ruined it." Not this soup.

Soak peas, lentils, or beans in 2 quarts water for 12 hours or overnight. Drain and put into big kettle. Add 12 cups water and ham bone or carcass. Bring to a boil, cover and simmer 3 hours. Add celery, carrots, parsley, salt, pepper, and paprika. Simmer 1 hour. Pick out bone or carcass. Put soup through a colander. Chill, then remove and set aside fat. Reheat soup, adding milk or cream. In small saucepan, melt 2 tablespoons of the reserved soup fat. Blend in the flour to make a smooth paste. Add a little soup to the paste, then stir all into soup pot, blending well. Serve soup very hot with corn bread. Serves 6.

2 cups dried peas, lentils, or beans
2 quarts cold water
1 ham bone or turkey carcass
12 cups water
1 cup chopped celery and leaves
1 cup chopped carrots
½ cup chopped parsley
1 teaspoon salt
½ teaspoon each black pepper and paprika
2 cups milk or cream
2 tablespoons flour
2 tablespoons soup fat

Menudo

Menudo is the peppery, garlicky, elixir-stew of Mexico, respected for its medicinal powers, especially recommended for hangover. Based on tripe, the stomach of the cow, the pig, or the sheep, and nixtamal (hominy), Menudo is an acquired taste.

Cut cleaned, thoroughly washed tripe into slices about 1 inch wide, and cook 1 hour in large pot with water. Add the hominy, without liquid if canned, and onion, garlic, salt, and marjoram. Simmer 6 to 7 hours. To serve, ladle into shallow plates; top with minced onions and hot, peppery, fresh salsa. Recipe serves 18 to 20 and freezes well (for emergency use).

5 cups tripe, well washed and trimmed
3 cups nixtamal, or canned hominy, drained
6 quarts water
2 onions, minced
4 cloves garlic, crushed and toasted
1 tablespoon salt
1 tablespoon marjoram (oregano)
minced green onions with tops
peppery salsa

Apache Acorn Soup

So important is the acorn to the Apache Indian's traditional way of life that one of the terms of the peace treaty made with the United States Government was an agreement that the Apaches forever will have the right to gather acorns on their hunting grounds. The nut of the oak is an Apache cooking basic. The outer part is not used; the acorn is peeled and ground. Originally cooked with venison or antelope, the soup today is most often beefed up.

2 to 3 pounds stewing beef
1 cup ground acorn meal
1 teaspoon salt
1 teaspoon pepper
2 quarts water

Cover beef with water and bring to a boil in heavy pot. Simmer several hours until well done, adding salt and pepper as meat cooks tender. Remove beef and chop on a flat stone until split in shreds. The meat broth continues to cook vigorously while meat and acorn flour (meal) are mixed together. Apaches stress their food is always well done: no instant cooking. Broth, meat, and meal simmer together until the broth bubbles creamy-white with yellow flecks, pleasantly acorn-scented and flavored.

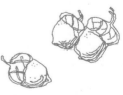

Chapter 3
Arizona-Mexican Foods and the Indispensable Chile

Mexican food, indigenous in tradition and heritage to the Arizona diet, has been hailed as the world's oldest cuisine by some.

Cortez found culinary gold when he conquered Montezuma: chocolate, peanuts, vanilla, pineapple, squash, sunflower seeds, guava, avocado, berries, the tomato, and the turkey.

Then there were beans. Not merely those which are tenderly refried, but black, fava, string, lima, pinto, and cocoa.

And little pods of chile flavor grew wild, in at least sixty varieties, all through Mexico. Originally *"chilli"* from the Nahuatl dialect of the Aztecs, the word was adopted into the Spanish vocabulary as *"chile"*.

In this chapter, chiles and the Mexican foods in which they are used are presented in historically proper fashion.

Chili, the seasoned powder, and chili con carne, the bowl of red ambrosia, are steaming in the next chapter.

By separating chiles and chili, I correct the impression that chili con carne is a Mexican dish. Chile con carne? Yes. Chili con carne, no.

Mexican food has been labeled colorful, fiery, capricious, nutritious, festive, and addictive. It is all that and more. Arizona possessed an early knowledge of its contrast, born of Indian-Hispanic roots in much of its territory. Until the Gadsden Purchase in 1854, Southern Arizona WAS Mexico.

Salsa, enchiladas, tacos, and their tasty cousins have been accepted so widely in the Southwest that many of the oldest Mexican dining places are owned or supervised by Lebanese, Syrians, Greeks, Germans, and Chinese. Not only have most ethnic groups adopted or adapted Mexican food, it has taken on a touch of statehood. We now have Cal-Mex, Tex-Mex, New Mexican, and, undisputably, Arizona-style Mexican food, Sonora based.

Jane Butel, in her Mexican food cook-

Continued on page 26

The original rooms of La Casa Córdova may well be the oldest surviving structure in Tucson, dating from prior to the Gadsen Purchase of 1854, when all Arizona below the Gila River was part of Mexico.

It is not known when the first rooms were built, but early property records indicate the land was owned by a prominent Hispanic pioneer, Teodoro Ramírez. Ramírez was born in Sonora, Mexico, in 1791, and moved with his parents to Tucson about 1812. The land apparently lay within the grounds of the Presidio de San Augustin del Tucson.

Gabino Ortega, who acquired the property in 1879 from Ramírez's niece, added three rooms and a zaguán (traditional Mexican doorway). With the original rooms, these make up La Casa Córdova as it exists today.

The building, now owned by the City of Tucson

and leased to the Tucson Museum of Art, takes its name from the Córdova family, which acquired it in 1936 and lived there from 1944 to 1973. On the Museum grounds, La Casa Córdova is one of the few Hispanic heritage museums in the United States. It is listed on the National Register of Historic Places. The courtyard, enclosed by an adobe wall, is landscaped with plants either native to Arizona or introduced from Mexico, and contains a ramada (thatched shed) and a raised platform equipped with comales (metal griddles) for cooking.

A major attraction at the museum is the annual Nacimiento presentation. A traditional Mexican nativity scene, the elaborate display contains more than two hundred hand-painted, miniature terra cotta figures.

Continued from page 24

books, credits Arizona with being as creative and innovative as California and much more so than Texas. Her studies (and mine) indicate Arizona is where the Topopo, the Sour Cream Enchilada, and the Chimichanga originated. John E. Mariani's *Dictionary of American Food and Drink* salutes Tucson as the original home of the "chimi." In Tucson, Carlotta Flores, whose roots go back to Maximilian's occupation, insists the melted-cheese flour tostado (Cheese Crisp) and Carne Seca originated there, too.

The Aztecs' tamales survived, almost intact, since the 1400s. Christmas Eve is still the night for family tamale making or giving. The Papago Indians, however, serve them only on All Souls' Day, when they place candles on family graves at twilight. Afterward, they go home to a simple tamale supper, leaving some on the table as sustenance for the souls who journey now in another world where corn and chile may not be available.

Food is one of the indispensable elements of any culture. Mexican food, then, is as complex as the history of its faces—from basic Indian to Spanish to French and German. Yet there is little snobbery in Mexican cooking. It is commonly based on corn, rice, beans, chile, and tomatoes, with cilantro and garlic for all.

Kearney Egerton, Southwestern historian and artist, wrote: "A fascinating thing about Mexico is how it absorbs a foreign influence into its national folk culture and makes it into something distinctively Mexican."

It is this sense of easy freedom and originality that should guide you through the use of chile peppers and these Mexican recipes. The smattering of examples is as varied as possible, each guaranteed to leave you with that inexplicable sense of well-being common to consumers of Mexican food and chiles.

Red Chile Powder

Purists are adamant about chile powder terms. Real chile powder is nothing but crushed, dried, red chile peppers. No additives, seasonings, or colorings. "Chili" powder, as sold in packets and shakers, is a blend we fuss over in the Chili chapter of this book.

How pure is pure Red Chile Powder? As pure as you please. Most cooks remove stems, seeds, and veins, which add heat, before grinding. Fearless veterans of this game grab a few dried pods off the *ristra* (string of dried chiles) and crush them in hand, filtering the dregs through the fingers as they add the pure powder to what they're cooking.

Because this is a heritage cookbook, I selected a no-nonsense recipe contributed to the *First Congregational Church Ladies Aid Society Cook Book* of 1909 by the dauntless Mrs. F. J. Steward, whose recipes filled several pages of "Mexican Cookery." She chose to roast her chiles in the oven before powdering them, which adds an extra taste dimension.

Red Chili (her spelling) Powder for Mexican Dishes

Clean thoroughly the red, dried chili peppers. Place in hot oven for a few minutes, then allow to cool. Crush to powder.

Red Chile Sauce

Wash dried whole chile pods. Wearing rubber gloves, remove stems and seeds. Cover with water and boil 30 minutes. Drain and put through a food mill or sieve. Heat lard in a heavy pan. Sauté onions and garlic. Add the flour and stir to make a smooth paste, slowly adding salt, oregano, and cumin. Combine with chile paste and thin with 1 cup tomato juice. Simmer ½ hour. (Some cooks thin sauce with 1 cup of water drained from chiles rather than tomato juice, adding depth of fire.) Either way, the yield is 2 cups. Combine with 1 pound round steak, trimmed and cubed. Cooked slowly, this makes classic chile con carne, red and robust.

24 dried red chiles
water to cover
2 onions, diced
2 cloves garlic, mashed
2 tablespoons lard
2 tablespoons flour
1 teaspoon salt
1 teaspoon each, oregano and cumin
1 cup tomato juice

Red Chile Paste

Red Chile Paste is the basis for many sauces and dishes, most commonly enchiladas and chile con carne. This recipe for paste and the method for sauce were culled from an old pink brochure on chiles, prepared by teaching home economists of the University of Arizona during pioneer days. (Most chiles never expected to make it to college.)

24 dried red chiles
2 tablespoons mashed garlic
1 teaspoon salt
2 quarts water or to cover

Wash whole dry chile pods. Wearing rubber gloves, remove stems, veins, and seeds. The pungency (fire) is in the seeds and veins; the amount to be removed is a cook's decision. Cover chiles with water in a kettle, bring to a boil, lower heat, and cook slowly 30 minutes. On a hot day or to save fuel, bring to a boil, remove from heat and cover, letting pods stand in hot water an hour. Drain. Put through colander or sieve after testing to make sure pulp separates easily from skin. To the resulting pulp, add garlic and salt. Blend smooth for a pure, thick chile paste.

To make Red Chile Sauce with Paste, simply add onions, garlic, lard, flour, salt, herbs, and tomato juice as in Sauce recipe. Freezes very well, covered.

Chiles, to Name a Few

The little wild pods of flavor that became the soul of Mexican food have been refined, given names and numbers, and scaled according to their abilities to bring tears, running noses, lip burning, and uncontrollable perspiration. Even so, confusion reigns. Example: the poblano chile in Arizona may be known as the pasilla in California and the pisado in Texas. This list in descending order of size may help the shopper-cook.

Big Jim: as much as 12 inches of large, firm mildness.
Anaheim or California: roughly 6 inches of usually mild and sweet, long, tapered chile.
New Mexico Green: fuller-bodied than Anaheim; fairly mild.
Poblano: round-shouldered and squatty; best for stuffing.
Ancho: dried poblano, almost square.
Jalapeño: waxy shorty; 2 to 4 inches of green heat.
Chipotle: jalapeño which has been smoke-dried to a diverse flavor.
Cayenne: several inches of burnout green; equally potent as the familiar dried red pepper powder.
Serrano: mucho hot, bright green, 1½ by ½ inches of wallop.
Chiletepin: buttons of bombs which induce gasping.

Chiles Verdes

When selecting green chiles *(chiles verdes)* for making salsa, you can choose your fire from fresh, canned, frozen, home-roasted, or broiled. The choice dictates the taste of the salsa.

Toss in several chiletepins, remembering these are choke-hot. Simmer 10 minutes with a dash of oregano as George Cockerham, a Phoenix fireman-cook, once taught me. Fight fire with fire.

Adding a tablespoon of olive oil reduces the bite of raw chiles. Adding a clove of crushed garlic adds pungency. Adding a small, juicy orange, peeled, and cut in bite-size pieces, plus freshly squeezed lemon juice to taste, creates a salsa to use as a dip with fresh fruit.

The easiest way to green chile wallop is through use of canned green chile peppers. Some say rinse and seed. Some say never rinse at all. Some say read the label: roasted are best. They are.

Macaria's Salsa de Chile Verde

Macaria Carlos, 70, gave me a lesson in roasting and saucing green chiles in the since-vanished town of Sonora, Arizona. As she made this cooked sauce, she recalled coming there in 1910. Prior to the Great Depression, more than 10,000 persons lived on the winding, one-way streets overlooking the giant open-pit copper mine. Below Sonora once was the town of Barcelona, named by its Spanish settlers. Before our visit, Macaria's son, Castro, had brought her a mound of shining fresh chiles from his grocery store. She roasted a few at a time on the comal *(griddle) and then put together a perfect salsa.*

10 green chiles, roasted and peeled
2 medium tomatoes, skinned
2 small cloves garlic
1 small onion
water and salt

Finely chop chiles, tomatoes, garlic, and onion. Put in saucepan with just enough water to cover ingredients, no more. Add a half-teaspoon of salt and simmer 10 minutes. To make it blistering, add a chopped green jalapeño chile, stemmed. Use this additive to separate the men from the boys.

Macaria also gave me an easy-to-remember formula for a quick, zesty, uncooked green salsa:

Five chile verde peppers to 1 good-size tomato to ½ a small onion, all ground or chopped together. Refrigerate.

Chile Colorado con Carne
(Red Chile)

Tony Gabaldon grew up in Northern Arizona eating and learning to cook authentic Mexican food, by his definition. When he became a state senator from Flagstaff, he fed the Senate and its secretaries red and green chile. During discussion of a bill outlawing labeling non-Indian arts as Indian made, Gabaldon proposed an amendment making it criminal to sell Mexican food that is not authentic. "And what's going to be authentic is my way," he chuckled. Included in the bill were his recipes for red and green chile. Persons selling chile made any other way would be prohibited from eating Mexican food "not less than one or more than three years."

The resulting furor caused Tony to withdraw the amendment on grounds "the bill was too hot to handle." That label never was officially tacked on his chile.

Trim any suet from meat, which may be beef or pork, or could be lamb. Render out fat in heavy skillet. Brown meat. Dice garlic and add. Stir in flour and brown. When brown, add red chile sauce and water. Cook 45 minutes. Add oregano and salt to taste. That's authentic. Frozen Chili Baca can be purchased in most southwestern grocery stores.

beef suet or fat from stew meat
2 pounds diced stew meat
2 small garlic cloves
4 tablespoons flour
8 ounces red chile sauce or frozen Red Chili Baca
1 quart water
oregano and salt to taste

Chile Verde con Carne
(Green Chile)

Tony Gabaldon's Green Chile is just as authentic as his Red Chile.

Brown meat and add diced garlic. Add flour and brown. Quickly add tomatoes. Chop (do not dice) green chiles and add. Stir to blend. Add water needed for consistency desired. Salt to taste. Cook 45 minutes.

2 pounds diced stew meat
2 small garlic cloves
4 tablespoons flour
1 7-ounce can stewed tomatoes
3 7-ounce cans Ortega whole green chiles
water
salt to taste

Chile Kellanada

Mexican cookery was an important section of the Bazar Cook Book, *published in 1909 by the Ladies Aid Society of the Tucson's First Congregational Church. Tucson, of course, was part of Mexico until the Gadsden Purchase of 1854. According to the Arizona Heritage Center's booklet,* The Mexican Legacy of Tucson, *throughout the rest of the Nineteenth Century Tucson grew from an outpost to a small but bustling metropolis. As Anglo capital and Anglo immigrants poured in, these newcomers relied much less on Hispanic partners or clientele.*

The cuisine, however, was another question, and the answer was wholehearted acceptance of the Mexican dishes so perfectly suited to the territory. I found it interesting that, in this church cookbook, all chile dishes have the "Chili" spelling. This recipe of Mrs. F. J. Steward's is the earliest I have found for stuffed chiles, now usually known as Chiles Rellenos. (It would be interesting to learn where the word "kellanada" came from.)

"Take green chili peppers, roast on top of stove, roll in cloth to steam until cold, then peel (after being steamed in this way, the skins are easily removed). Cut off tops. Scoop out carefully to remove seeds and veins and fill with mixture made of grated Mexican cheese, chopped olives, chopped onion. Dip in egg and cracker meal and fry in hot lard as you would oysters. Serve hot."

Incredibly Easy Chile Rellenos

For years I avoided making chile rellenos for company, because, although they tasted fine, their appearance left much to be desired. Then Eloise Hayt, whose knowledge of Mexican cuisine was demonstrated at her many dinners for fellow members of the Maricopa County Bar Auxiliary, showed me how to make perfect pans of these tender, triple-threat (chiles, cheese, and eggs) guest pleasers.

Wash chiles and remove seeds. Wrap chile strips around cheese strips. Place side by side in a shallow, 13 by 9-inch baking dish. Beat eggs with salt, then add milk and mix well. Pour over stuffed chiles. Bake 50 to 60 minutes in a 350-degree oven. Do *not* overbake, since it toughens the protein in both eggs and cheese. Serves 6 to 8.

1 large (27-ounce) can green chile strips
1 pound sharp cheddar cheese, in strips
12 eggs
½ teaspoon salt
1½ cups milk

Tostadas and Nachos

As Mexican food captured the Southwest, the same dish appeared in different regions wearing differing names. In the Tucson area, tostadas were the classical beginning to a meal: large flour tortillas, first served hot and plain—later, liberally sizzling with melted cheese. They are still ordered as Cheese Tostadas de Harina. In Phoenix, they are ordered as Cheese Crisps. Time was when nachos and tostadas were merely crisply fried corn tortillas, broken into quarters to be used as chips or scoops for salsa, refried beans, or guacamole. In Phoenix, they were usually referred to as "corn chips".

Nachos today have evolved into chips loaded with melted cheeses and jalapeño slices, a dish unknown in heritage days. Should anyone be ambitious enough to home-fry a nacho, here's how.

Heat lard to French-fry temperatures of 390 degrees. Drop torn tortilla pieces into hot fat, a few at a time. Remove with slotted spoon. Drain on paper towels. Sprinkle with salt or cheese and serve at once. Oven-melt the cheese if desired. Serve either with salsa at room temperature.

1 cup lard or shortening
4 or 5 corn tortillas
salt or cheese

Editor's note: See pages 54-55 for tortilla recipes.

Tacos

The classic Taco of Arizona is a crisply fried corn tortilla filled with seasoned beef, the corn shell folded to a half-moon shape. There are also soft and rolled tacos and crisp and rolled tacos called Flautas. Crisp and flat tacos are most often spread with refried beans and known as Bean Tostadas. If this recipe looks lengthy for a Beef Taco, remember that taco means "wad" or "mouthful."

Fry corn tortillas, one at a time, in less than an inch of hot lard or oil, keeping them curved or U-shaped, rather than V-shaped. Use kitchen tongs to hold one side while frying or use a taco maker, a metal mold. Drain on paper and keep warm. To make filling, combine meat, onions, peppers, and seasonings, browning slowly. Stir often. Divide meat filling among taco shells, then top with lettuce, tomato, avocado, and cheese. Serve with taco sauce—which will always be too mild for some guests and too hot for others. Tacos also come with chicken, turkey, ham, vegetable, and machaca (dried spiced beef) fillings.

8 corn tortillas
1½ pounds coarse-ground beef
1 small onion, finely chopped
1 canned green chile, diced
1 teaspoon red chile powder
1 clove garlic, finely minced
½ teaspoon oregano
½ teaspoon cumin
1 teaspoon salt
3 cups lettuce, shredded
1 ripe tomato, diced
1 large avocado, diced
2 cups chedder cheese, shredded
taco sauce
lard or oil for frying

Sandra's Cream Taco Casserole

This popular baked dish became more commonly served than the previously most used "Mexican" standby, Tamale Pie. Sandra Day O'Connor's version—smooth, piquant, with real cream, not canned mushroom soup—became a favorite and appeared in many Arizona cookbooks. Some felt she could have run for President on the Cream Taco platform but the United States Supreme Court intervened.

Dip tortillas in hot oil just to soften. Drain and cool on paper towels or paper bag. Salt tortillas and tear into quarters. Set aside. Sauté chopped onion in remaining oil. Add the cream—skim milk will never give the desired satiny sauce— to stir over low heat 5 minutes. Add chiles and taco sauce and stir to blend. Have ready a buttered, 2-quart casserole. Layer into it the torn tortillas, chicken, sauce, and cheese, in that order. Bake, uncovered, about 45 minutes at 350 degrees. Serves 6. This is a rousing way to use up leftover turkey.

12 corn tortillas
2 tablespoons corn oil
salt
1 onion, finely chopped
1½ cups light cream or half-and-half
4 ounces diced green chiles
½ cup taco sauce
butter
3 cups cooked, diced chicken
8 ounces sharp cheddar cheese, grated

Enchiladas

Enchiladas are heaven on a plate when lavishly sauced and baked until the corn tortilla swells to mealiness, topped with an assertive cheese and subdued onion. Mrs. Ed Barragan of Clarkdale sent this recipe to Abbie Keith, beloved editor of The Arizona Cattlelog.

Prepare sauce by browning flour in hot shortening, then adding red chile sauce and water. (Canned enchilada sauce is now available.) Let sauce simmer as each tortilla is lightly fried just long enough to soften. Dip each quickly into sauce. Place flat in baking dish. Spread with diced onion, cheese, and a touch of oregano. Roll up and arrange, seam side down, placing close together until dish is filled. Pour sauce over all and sprinkle with more cheese and onion. Place in hot oven long enough to steam tortillas and melt cheese. Allow at least two each per person, garnishing plate with lettuce, radishes, and olives. Or olives may be baked with enchiladas.

Stacked enchiladas were the preference for many families, 3 layers to a stack. Crisp, flat-fried tortillas were dipped into sauce, then stacked on a plate with one or more fillings between each layer: refried beans, grated cheese and onion, cooked meat. These were usually topped with a fried or steamed egg.

12 corn tortillas
shortening
1 tablespoon flour
2 cups red chile sauce
¼ cup water
1 diced onion
1 cup grated cheese
oregano
sliced ripe olives
shredded lettuce and radishes

Cherry Valley Baked Burritos

Harry Hendrickson, whose uncle designed the noted La Fonda Hotel in Santa Fe, built a somewhat smaller home in Cherry Valley's reddish humps south of Oracle. Edna Mae, his wife, was a noted cook and the Oracle School librarian; Harry was a supervisor for Magma Copper Company. Edna Mae built a better burro. "Fat cigar size," she said. "Small enough to be called burritos."

Brown meat in skillet, then add taco sauce and simmer until meat is well done. Taste and add seasoning if needed. Butter a casserole or baking pan large enough to hold 2 dozen fat cigars. Place tortilla in pan, spoon generous tablespoon of meat mixture in tortilla center and top with thin strip of cheese. Roll up, tuck ends in place, seam down, in baking dish. Repeat until all tortillas are filled and in place. Brush with melted butter and bake 30 minutes at 350 degrees. Serve with refried beans and green vegetable salad. Serves 6 to 8 happily.

2 pounds lean ground beef
2 cups taco sauce
salt and pepper, if necessary
1 pound jack cheese, in strips
2 dozen 6-inch flour tortillas
butter

Irrigation made the Arizona desert flourish. The U.S. Reclamation Service's canal system watered this lettuce crop in the Yuma area about 1915. ARIZONA HISTORICAL SOCIETY, YUMA

Chimichangas

Chimichanga is a word which is said to have no meaning in the Spanish or any Indian language. In English, to most Mexican food addicts, a Chimichanga is a flour tortilla stuffed with meat, beans, and cheese in some combination, deep-fried, then topped with copious amounts of guacamole, sour cream, more cheese, and lettuce and tomato garnish.

John E. Mariani's Dictionary of American Food and Drink salutes Tucson as the original home of the "chimi." Tucson is sure of that. The question is: Who first put one together and when?

Carlotta Flores, whose family has owned El Charro Mexican Restaurant since 1922, insists that not only the Chimichanga but also the melted cheese flour tostada originated there. Her aunt, Monica Flin, a Tucson legend, ran the kitchen for 54 years.

John Fennings, of The Tucson Daily Citizen, conducted an ongoing quest for the chimi facts. The jury is out. Lucy Mesa claimed she invented it in a Nogales restaurant, La Frontera. Club 21 said they put it on the menu first. Joe Lancaster wrote that when he worked on the railroad, it was common to heat burros on a stick over a campfire for lunch. Claims keep coming. This recipe came to me from Judith England, who was born on the family ranch near Magdalena, Sonora, Mexico. She and husband Gene owned an illustrious business, their Santa Cruz Chili Company, in Amado, Arizona, since 1938.That's authentic enough for me.

2 tablespoons corn oil plus ½ cup oil
1 cup chopped meat, cooked tender
1 medium onion, diced
3 canned tomatoes
4 drained pimentos, diced
1 large cold, boiled, diced potato
2 large green chile peppers, seeded and diced
½ teaspoon crushed oregano
8 medium flour tortillas, 10-inch
8 strips sharp cheese

Judy neatly fielded the meat question by suggesting "meat of choice, beef, pork, goat, or game," but tender. Heat 2 tablespoons of oil and add all ingredients but tortillas, cheese, and ½ cup oil. Mix ingredients gently to blend vegetables and meat, cooking until oregano flavor is thoroughly absorbed. Place 2 tablespoons meat filling on each tortilla, fold in sides, and roll to close like an envelope. Brown in small amount of remaining oil, hot. No need to deep fry for a crisp crust; just brown with attention. Top each with a strip of cheese and allow to melt before serving with red or green salsa. They agree with railroader Joe Lancaster, who said, "As for the person who slopped sour cream on a Chimichanga, or any Mexican food, I use a cowboy phrase, 'Get a rope.' "

Tamales

These are not cocktail party tamales, but the traditional family recipe used to make about 12 dozen big, cornhusk-wrapped bundles from the welcoming kitchen of Mrs. Felicitas Fontes of Ray. "This is a good way to use venison or other game," she advised. Mrs. Fontes' garden and kitchen were swallowed up by development of the open-pit mine.

Chile Mixture: Brown flour in 1 tablespoon lard very lightly and add the red chile paste and tomato juice. Simmer a minute.

Meat Mixture: Simmer chuck in water to cover until tender, adding 2 or 3 garlic cloves, salt, and peppercorns for flavor. Shred the meat and reserve the broth.

Masa Mixture: Beat pork lard by hand or mixer until creamy. In a large wooden bowl combine the masa, creamed lard, the chile mixture, and meat broth. Add salt to season. Dough should not be runny, but the consistency of cookie dough.

Wash cornhusks in very hot water and pat dry. Spread thin layer of masa dough on cornhusk, leaving margin on sides and pointed end clear. In center of dough place shredded meat. Roll from side and fold over pointed end. Steam in a large container with a rack, stacking the tamales in staggered rows so the steam can permeate thoroughly. Cook on very low heat 1½ hours, checking to make sure there is water for steam, beginning with 3 cups. Tamales freeze and resteam to perfection.

1 tablespoon flour
1 tablespoon lard
1 quart red chile paste
10 ounces tomato juice
6 pounds boneless chuck
2 or 3 garlic cloves
salt
peppercorns
3 pounds pork lard
8 pounds Masa Harina
cornhusks, soaked

More Tamales, Please!

To make a tamale is a labor of love, born in tradition. The Aztecs invented it—a woman, no doubt; maybe the homemaker's club. The word comes from the Nahuatl, *tamili*. Although the Aztecs had an advanced civilization before Cortez conquered them in 1519, their passion for both breakfast and dinner tamales may explain Cortez's victory. Tamales take undivided time. Someone had to pick the corn, shell it, boil it, grind it into meal, and then beat it into dough—before filling it to cook. The Aztecs were conquered but the tamale survived and was put together the same painstaking way for another 400 years. At least they come in their own plate, once unfolded, and no eating utensils are necessary.

By the time this food writer encountered the tamale in Arizona, food choppers and meat grinders, steamers, and the production of Masa Harina eased the tamale production burden. It still takes time and is well worth it. For hundreds of Arizona families in town kitchens, on ranches and reservations, no Christmas Eve is complete without tamales.

Carneseca con Arroz

This simple recipe from a collection gathered by St. Ann's Catholic Parish about 1909 shows that Tucson ladies, as well as village cooks, pounded Carneseca (their spelling as one word).

"Wash one dozen pieces of ranch-dried beef, toast in the oven until crisp, pound until meat is thoroughly separated, have ready a skillet with two tablespoons of hot fat, put in pounded meat, sprinkle with two tablespoons (small) of flour, when flour is browned add boiling water enough to cover, salt, a clove of garlic, tomatoes, onion, green chilis, if preferred. [One sentence and that's it!] Cook ¾ cup of rice in 2 cups salted water, arrange about platter when cooked, pouring stewed meat in center, serve."

Again, admirable brevity.

12 pieces ranch beef
2 tablespoons hot fat
2 tablespoons flour
boiling water
salt
1 clove garlic
tomatoes
onions
green chiles
¾ cup rice
2 cups salted water

Carne Seca

After visiting with cooks all over the state for a dozen years, it became apparent that there is a sort of food Mason-Dixon Line in Arizona. It is marked roughly by the Gila River. South of the Gila, Sonoran cooking and customs still have the strong influence, more than 100 years after the Gadsden Purchase.

There is a marked difference in Mexican food as served in restaurants. If the food is much the same, the menu term may be different. Lean, fire-browned, subtly seasoned beef north of the Gila is usually called Carne Machaca. South it becomes Carne Seca, especially when sun-dried in the historic way. They refer to Northern and Central Arizona machaca as "stew meat" and, truthfully, it is always juicier and often less flavorful than the Carne Seca of Tucson, Douglas, Nogales, and Yuma. All methods of drying meat have improved, however.

The United States Bureau of American Ethnology Annual Report of 1892-1893 stated: "Jerky is fresh meat cut in thin strips, stripping off the tallow, cured by air. Spanish jerky, called Carne Seca, is highly seasoned with vinegar, black pepper and a little salt before drying. Sometimes it is rubbed with garlic and sprinkled with red chili."

In the *Mission Cook Book* of 1909, a recipe for Carneseca con Arroz appeared, which proves that as late as that date, kitchen duty demanded strength and endurance.

Carne Machaca

Carne Machaca, which means "battered meat" in Spanish, was originally the term for a method by which Carne Seca (dried meat) was made more chewable. At the Arizona Heritage Center, I learned that the Mexican housewife early in her kitchen career went to the nearest stream bed and selected two smooth stones; one large and flat enough to hold the dried strips of meat, the other round or oval, comfortable for pounding. What a well-adjusted, happy woman she must have been—pounding out her frustrations on the dried meat just as she crushed her problems grinding chiles in the molcajete.

Eventually, mamacita made the happy discovery that slow cooking coupled with lime juice and spices made dry meat tender. This method, coupled with oven browning, resulted in the Carne Machaca found in most Mexican homes and restaurants. This is my composite of many recipes.

Heat 2 tablespoons bacon drippings in heavy kettle or Dutch oven. Sear beef (or game) on all sides, then season. Add just enough hot water to cover bottom of pan. Cook, covered, until very tender. With 2 forks, pull meat into strings, then cut into bite-sized pieces. Doing this in pan allows the juices to further flavor meat.

In large, heavy skillet, heat the remaining bacon fat and sauté onion, garlic, tomatoes, and chiles. Add Carne Machaca and correct seasonings, if needed. Sprinkle with lime juice. Cook, covered, for 15 minutes. Uncover and continue cooking, stirring thoroughly at times until meat is browned and dry, but tender. Enough for 10 burros or 20 tacos de luxe.

For Machaca Burros, warm flour tortillas of any size. Spread with meat in center, roll up, and eat like a sandwich. For Machaca Tacos, spoon meat into taco shells.

3 pounds brisket, flank, or rump
¼ cup bacon drippings
salt & pepper
hot water
1 medium onion, chopped
1 clove garlic, chopped
2 tomatoes, diced
4-ounce can green chiles, diced
1 tablespoon fresh lime juice

Corn Tortillas are a work of art in the hands of an experienced tortilla maker. A tortilla press works well for the inexperienced. In either case, cooking is done best on a hot Comal *(griddle).* ARIZONA HIGHWAYS COLLECTION

Chorizo

During one of the annual Friendly House Tamale Suppers in Phoenix, served to bolster funds for the education of the foreign-born who are helped there, I tasted this robust sausage. I begged the recipe. This Chorizo keeps down to the last bite—it must be the pound of dried chile peppers. Chorizo is the basis for many distinctive Mexican treats, and a worthy companion to Huevos Rancheros—breakfast eggs zipped with salsa on a corn tortilla.

Soak chile peppers and pork in vinegar overnight. Next day, remove the chiles and grind them to a paste with the garlic, salt, and seasonings. Drain the meat thoroughly and place in bowl. With your fingers or a wooden paddle, blend the chile paste with the pork until very well mixed. Stuff into sausage casings and tie the ends. This recipe should make 6 sausages.

In the days before refrigerators, the sausages were hung in the hot sun for 3 days before using or storing. Today you can just refrigerate them until you're ready to use them. For long-term storage, put them in the refrigerator or freezer.

Instead of stuffing the Chorizo into casings, you may simply use it in bulk form, or make into patties.

1 pound dry red chile peppers
6 pounds lean pork, ground fine
1 cup white or cider vinegar
6 cloves garlic
salt to taste
1 teaspoon ground cumin
1 teaspoon marjoram
1 pinch sugar
sausage casings

Huevos Rancheros

Ranch eggs, Mexican style, are a rousing departure from most Anglo breakfast eggs. They fire from the whites of the yi's.

Heat oil in a skillet just a bit larger than the corn tortillas. Fry each tortilla tender-crisp, about 30 seconds per side. Drain each and keep warm in paper towels or clean flour sack. Discard all but a trace of any remaining oil and reduce heat to warm. Have the shelled eggs ready to slip into pan without breaking yolks. Cook only until whites are set, seasoning with salt and pepper to taste. Place quickly 1 egg per tortilla and keep warm while just as quickly heating salsa in pan, stirring. Pour over eggs. Top with cheese, which will melt invitingly as eggs are served. Ideally, the breakfast plate comes with hot refried beans and a small mound of Chorizo (Mexican sausage). Serves 2 to 4.

4 corn tortillas
2 or 3 tablespoons corn or olive oil
4 eggs
salt and pepper
1 cup red or green chile salsa
½ cup shredded white or longhorn cheese

Joe's Posole

Joe Burgoz grew up on a farm near Parker on the Arizona side of the Colorado River. "I loved to cook. I was always in mama's apron strings," he recalled after winning blue ribbons for cooking chili, salsa, menudo, and this Posole. And the Posole gets better as it ages.

Parboil 4 pounds of lean, country-style ribs in unsalted water. Meanwhile, in large skillet, melt lard and sauté onion and garlic with cumin and oregano. Pour into rib pot. Stir. Add hominy and beans, then chile sauce, and stir convincingly. Taste for salt. Add, if needed, then cook 1 hour, covered. Serves 8 and sticks awhile.

4 pounds lean pork ribs
2 quarts water
2 tablespoons lard
1 large onion, chopped
2 cloves garlic, crushed
1 pinch cumin
1 teaspoon oregano
29-ounce can of hominy, drained
6 cups cooked pinto beans, seasoned
1 cup red chile sauce
salt, if needed

Frijoles

As indispensable as corn is the bean to the Mexican diet. the runner bean is traceable in the Tamaulipas Mountains area of Mexico back to 7000 B.C. With instinctive wisdom, early cooks combined beans and corn tortillas, which provides tasty and economically, complete protein. Beans, with corn and chiles, became the third staple of Mexico.

In Spanish, beans are "frijoles," a name commonly used by early settlers in Arizona and found often in turn-of-the-century cookbooks. The red bean or the pinto (speckled like the horse) bean were the most commonly grown in Arizona-Sonora territory. Not merely the name, frijoles, but the Mexican method of adding zest to the beanpot was adopted. This recipe is from the Mission Cook Book *of St. Ann's Catholic Church in Tucson, produced in 1909, reprinted just as written, usable today.*

red or spanish beans
1 tablespoon sweet oil
1 small chopped onion
finely chopped chili peppers, to taste
salt, to taste

"Boil a cupful of red or Spanish beans until soft, several hours before using, setting them aside to cool in the water they were boiled in. Put a tablespoon of sweet oil or very nice dripping into a frying pan. Add a small chopped onion and, before it browns, add the beans, together with more of the water in which they were boiled. Season liberally with salt and with finely chopped chili peppers, as they should be decidedly hot. Mash them as they cook, adding more water from time to time, so they will not be too dry. Cook until thoroughly heated."

Elma's Green Rice

When Elma married Paul Jones Fannin, she was destined to hostess occasions beyond her wildest dreams. From Stanford University sports figure to successful family business-man to, eventually, Governor of Arizona and United States Senator, the tireless Fannin always had Elma at his side. And she often had Green Rice as her kitchen standby, one of the dishes Arizona newcomers called "Mexican food" because of the chiles.

Add olive oil to cooked rice in large bowl and mix well. Add remaining ingredients except eggs. Stir to blend. Beat eggs and add, stirring well. Pour into 2-quart buttered casserole. Bake 1 hour at 350 degrees. Serves 10. "This is extremely good as a leftover blessing," Elma recommended. For very hot rice, use 2 cans of green chiles.

2 cups cooked long-grain rice
⅔ cup olive oil
1 clove garlic, chopped
1 medium bell pepper, diced
1 medium onion, chopped
½ cup parsley, minced
4-ounce can green chiles, diced
2 jars (3-ounce) pimento cheese spread
1 cup sliced mushrooms
13-ounce can evaporated milk
2 cups grated sharp cheese
2 eggs

Almendrado

The Spanish, after a few chile dishes, were quick to introduce soothing gelatin desserts into New Spain. Always inventive with color, Mexico responded with Almendrado, a delicate, sauced gelatin dessert tinted red, white, and green, the colors of their flag.

Soften gelatin in cold water. Add boiling water and dissolve. Cool. Beat egg whites stiff, adding sugar slowly, alternating with the cool gelatin liquid. Add vanilla, almond extract, and salt. Whip thoroughly to foaming peak stage. Divide mixture into 3 parts. Fold ground almonds into one. Tint the others a soft green and a delicate red. Spoon red layer into 9 by 5 by 3-inch loaf pan, then white almond layer, then green. Refrigerate at least 4 hours. Slice to serve in squares, swimming in sauce.

Almendrado Sauce: Dissolve 2 tablespoons cornstarch in 1 tablespoon cold milk. Add to 2 cups scalded milk. Boil and stir to thicken slightly. Beat egg yolks not used in gelatin with ½ teaspoon vanilla and ½ teaspoon almond extract. Slowly add to hot mixture. Simmer until sauce coats a spoon; takes only minutes. Chill. Spoon generously over Almendrado, topped with toasted almonds. Serves 8 to 10.

1½ envelopes gelatin
½ cup cold water
¼ cup boiling water
6 egg whites
½ cup sugar
1 teaspoon vanilla
½ teaspoon almond extract
½ cup ground almonds
pinch of salt
red and green food coloring

Buñuelos
(Fried Fritters)

Buñuelos (fried fritters or cookies) and Sopapillas (fried pillows of bread) and Indian fry bread are similar but not the same. Buñuelos are a traditional Christmas season sweet, originally shaped over a napkin-covered kneecap.

In a large bowl, beat eggs, then beat in butter and milk. Combine flour, sugar, and salt and add to egg mixture. Mix well. Turn dough out on a lightly floured board and knead until silky smooth but not sticky. Divide dough into about 12 to 14 pieces and shape into little balls. Cover and let rest for about 20 minutes. Roll each out into a circle, very thin. Let rest another 5 minutes, then fry one at a time in hot oil until pale gold. Drain on paper. Make a thin syrup by adding a little hot water to a cone of Mexican brown sugar *(piloncillo)* or to ¼ cup brown sugar with a dash of cloves. Stir with cinnamon sticks, allowing syrup to cool a bit with cinnamon. Use syrup as a dip or trickle over buñuelos.

2 eggs
2 tablespoons melted butter
¼ cup milk
2 cups flour
1 tablespoon sugar
1 teaspoon salt
oil or lard for frying
brown sugar syrup
cinnamon sticks

Flan

Silky, soothing Flan (custard) is known as Mexico's national dessert. My husband loved custard; therefore, he loved Mexico. No matter where we kilometered though that always surprising land—vintage trucks hurtling toward us, skeletal cows hovering in our path—we could count on one comforting thing. The tiniest cafe, the most bare-bones roadstop, always had Flan—invariably made with canned milk and caramelized with panocha, little pillows of raw brown sugar, and fragrant with Mexican vanilla. This recipe of Dena Zepeda Wood's is more elegant than roadside Flan.

Put 1 cup of sugar into square, flame-proof pan in which custard will be baked. Place over heat, stirring until sugar melts and turns golden. Remove and tip until pan is coated with caramel. Cool. Beat egg whites to a froth. Beat yolks to foam, then beat together. Add milk, remaining sugar, and vanilla. Beat until sugar dissolves. Strain custard into caramel-coated pan. Cover with plastic wrap. Place in larger pan containing an inch of hot water. Bake 1 hour at 350 degrees. While hot, turn out on warm serving platter. Chill. When serving, pour brandy or rum over flan and ignite. Bring to table flaming. Serves 8.

1 ¾ cups sugar
3 eggs, separated
2 cans (13-ounce) evaporated milk
2 teaspoons vanilla
2 tablespoons rum or brandy

Chapter 4
Chili:
Incendiary and Evolutionary

Chili, basically, is heat and meat. This chapter points out what is, and is not, chili.

Chili is a bowl of red, colored—not by tomato—but by the scarlet pod of *capsicum frutescens,* the chile pepper.

Chili is not a Mexican food.

Eating in America, written by Waverly Root and Richard de Rochemont, put it bluntly, "One Mexican dictionary goes so far as to define chili con carne as a 'detestable food with a false Mexican title which is sold in the United States from Texas to New York.' "

In Arizona, it is not detestable and has fired our history from Army and stagecoach days to Senator Barry Goldwater's victory as Chili Champion of the United States Senate.

In between, small wars waged—and continue. Is real chili full of beans? What kind of beans? Which cut of meat? Ground or chunked? Should the heat come from chili powder, chiles powdered, or both?

In this book, the chile pepper is dealt with in the chapter on Mexican food. Researching old cookbooks and papers, I found early Arizona dubbed anything with chiles a 'chili' dish. Today, the purists spell most chile dishes with an 'e'.

A study of the chili recipes that follow lines up with H. Allen Smith, humorist who devoted the latter part of his life to a study of chilimania. "Chili, the dish, is chili in the United States of America. Chile, the pepper, is chile everywhere," he pronounced.

Chil*e* is made chil*i* by chile, I add—with meat, whether antelope, javelina, or beef. In the dish, or on the side, the bean is Chili con Carne's best friend.

One historian called it "the mess wagon of the cow country." Before the chuck wagon, every cowboy had to carry his own grub, bedroll, and everything else he needed to sustain himself on the trail. The chuck wagon not only freed him in this regard, but it came to be the "social center of the roundup and the meeting place for any riders scattered on the trail drive," according to historian Peter Watts.

Charles Goodnight, Texas Ranger, famed cattleman, and developer of the Goodnight-Loving Trail, generally is credited with the concept of building a chuck box into an old, iron-axled, former Army wagon. In the classic design, the door of the chuck box served as the wagon's tailgate. With hinged legs, it let down to become a work surface for the cook, and provide

access to shelves, drawers, and chuck. Bedrolls were stowed in the wagon, and the boot—a cowhide slung from axle to axle beneath the wagon bed—carried skillets, Dutch ovens, firewood, and other heavy items.

Along with a well-stocked chuck wagon came the "uncrowned king" of the outfit, the range cook. Cowman John M. Hendrix, quoted in Cattleman, *said: "He was conscious of his autocratic powers, and his crankiness is still traditional." Ramon F. Adams wrote in agreement: "Only a fool argues with a skunk, a mule, or a cook."*

In modern-day Arizona and throughout the West, the chuck wagon mostly contributes atmosphere to tenderfoot trail rides and cookouts.

Juniper House Chili Menu

The overwhelming popularity of chili was illustrated by this menu from the grand opening of the Juniper House, a combination hotel and restaurant in Prescott. Fittingly, it began operations July 4, 1864.

George W. Barnard was the owner, operator, and sole kitchen staff, so customers were entrusted to pay their own checks as they went out. Whether it was the fiscal policy or the chili, the Juniper House eventually folded.

Breakfast
Fried venison and chili
Bread and coffee with milk

Dinner
Roast venison and chili
Chili and baked beans
Chili on tortillas
Tea and coffee with milk

Supper
Chili, from 4 o'clock on

Chili Powder

Chili powder is uniquely American even though its basic ingredients are the flavor zingers of Mexican food: chile pods, cumin, oregano, garlic, onion, salt, and sometimes allspice or cilantro.

Mexican cooks use these ingredients in separate portions. Legend has it that the mixture we know as chili powder was created in Texas. Some say an Englishman who had lived in India was trying to mix up curry powder. Others credit a German immigrant with developing chili powder in New Braunfels, Texas, in 1902. Barry Goldwater traced chili to Algiers. Ted De Grazia accepted the legend of old Papago storytellers that Maria de Jesus de Agreda, the Blue Lady, brought chili to the Indians. Ponder the legends, then pick one for your own story-spinning while you mix a batch of chili powder.

4 Anaheim chiles, dried
1 pequin chile, dried, optional
2 teaspoons cumin seed, dried
1 teaspoon oregano, dried
½ teaspoon garlic powder
1 teaspoon onion salt

Stem and seed the chiles with care. Do not rub eyes and do not use pequin chile unless you are a hothead. Combine and pulverize with remaining ingredients in a molcajete (volcanic stone bowl) or blender. Store in airtight container. Additional flavor can be added with a dash of fresh ground cloves or allspice.

Early Chili or Picadillo

The Mission Cook Book *compiled by St. Ann's Society of Tucson in 1909, contained the Gonzales family version of Chili con Carne, also called Picadillo. Fancier versions of Picadillo add raisins, olives, and wine.*

Grind raw or cooked meat with onion. Have the lard very hot in heavy skillet. Add meat and sprinkle at once with flour, salt, and pepper. While this is browning on medium heat, combine chili powder with boiling water and let boil. When meat is brown, add chili water and stir. Reduce heat to low and let stew until ready to heat, adding the tomatoes if this flavor is desired. In either case, Picadillo is good with beans or rice in the bowl. Serves 4 with beans or rice.

1 pound beefsteak, raw or cooked
1 onion, diced
2 tablespoons lard
1 tablespoon flour
salt and black pepper to taste
1 tablespoon chili powder
1 pint boiling water
½ cup tomatoes, if desired

Stagecoach Chili

The famed Butterfield Stage offered the cold and weary or the hot and jittery some form of chili year around during trips through Southern Arizona. If game or beef was at hand, it was Chili con Carne. If not, Chili Beans and, at worst, Chili Soup. Historians Roscoe Willson and Will James both wrote colorfully of those fly-infested, open-air way stations. This chili is not for sissies or children.

Toast chiles in hot skillet. Then boil a half-hour in water with garlic. Cool and strain through sieve, making a chili paste rather than the usual chili powder. Sauté onion with salt pork. Sprinkle cumin and oregano over meat (antelope, bear, venison, or wild pig will do if beef is not available) and brown with salt pork and onion. Add chili paste and tomatoes. Stir to blend and simmer 1 hour. Taste and add salt and pepper as needed. Simmer at least another 20 minutes before serving. It's better and hotter the second day. This recipe is why chili is called "red hot." Serve with pinto beans cooked with onion and garlic, and biscuits.

10 dried red chiles
2 cloves garlic, diced
4 cups water
2 onions, chopped fine
1 tablespoon salt pork, diced
1 teaspoon cumin powder
½ teaspoon oregano
2 or 3 cups chopped game or beef
1 cup chopped tomatoes, if available
salt and black pepper

Barry Goldwater's Arizona Chili

Not since Theodore Roosevelt has there been a Republican who has combined more action in more varied fields than Barry Goldwater. River runner, photographer, prolific writer, and jet pilot, he colorfully represented Arizona in Washington, never more humorously than at the Senatorial Chili Cookoffs. When he triumphantly carried away the championship blowtorch, he promised, "Next year, I'll make this stuff tonight look like what you scrape out of hen houses." His recipe has been cooked for countless charitable events. He belongs to the chili-and-beans group.

Sauté beef and drain off excess fat, leaving a little for flavor. Add beans, puree, and onion and stir well. Mix the chili powder, cumin, and salt (about 2 teaspoons to his taste) and add to chili. Bring to a boil, stirring. Turn low and cook slowly until onions and beans are tender, adding water to desired consistency as needed. Serves 4 to 6 guests who know beans about chili.

1 pound dry pinto beans, soaked overnight
1 pound coarse-ground beef
6 ounces tomato puree
2 cups chopped onion
3 tablespoons chili powder
1 tablespoon cumin
salt to taste
water, as needed

Hot Tamale Pie

Hot Tamale Pie, like Chili con Carne, sounds Mexican but is really this-side-of-the-border food. Mrs. Ernest W. McFarland, wife of the former Governor of Arizona, compiled a book of Congressional wives' recipes when her husband served as a Senator. An excellent cook, she was known for this mush crust pie, a giant tamale in a casserole.

Grind meat, then combine with meat stock, garlic, onion, chili powder, comino, and salt. Cook for 15 minutes. Stir in olives. Make a stiff mush by scalding cornmeal with boiling water, 1 tablespoon salt. Line a baking dish with the mush, reserving enough for topping. Pour the meat mixture into bottom crust. Make a top crust of remaining mush. Bake to a golden brown, 45 minutes at 345 degrees. Serves 6.

2 cups cooked beef or pork
1½ cups meat stock
1 garlic clove, minced
1 large onion, chopped
2 tablespoons chili powder
1 cup pitted ripe olives
½ teaspoon ground comino seed
salt to taste
1 pound cornmeal
3 cups boiling water
1 tablespoon salt

Wherever the chuck wagon set up became the focal point of the cowboy's life when he was not in the saddle. Food was important, and cookie was catered to, on the Greene Cattle Company spread in Santa Cruz County.
ARIZONA HISTORICAL SOCIETY, TUCSON

Sallie Hayden's Chili

The Hayden Flour Mills in early Tempe, well situated by the Hayden Ferry on the Salt River, bagged beans as well as grain products. Sallie Hayden's Chili was a civilized blend of meat and spices with, of course, the family brand of beans.

Wash and pick over beans. Soak in fresh water overnight. Drain. Cover with 1 quart fresh water and salt, then simmer in heavy 4-quart kettle 1½ hours. Sauté bacon and drain on towel. Brown beef or venison in drippings. Add to beans with seasonings, tomato puree, and beef broth. Sauté onion and pepper in butter to add to beans. Cover, simmer until beans are tender, about 3 hours. Garnish with crumbled bacon. Serves 6 - 8.

2 cups Rose Brand pinto or red beans
1 quart fresh water
1 tablespoon salt
4 slices bacon
1 pound chopped beef or venison
2 tablespoons bacon drippings
2 cloves garlic, crushed
1 ½ cups tomato puree
1 cup beef broth
4 teaspoons chili powder
½ teaspoon oregano
¼ teaspoon each, sage and cumin seed
2 tablespoons butter
2 cups onion, chopped
½ green chile pepper, seeded and diced

The chuck wagon freed cowboys from the necessity of carrying their own grub and bedrolls on the trail or on roundups. It also meant better eating and a place to congregate and socialize.
ARIZONA HISTORICAL SOCIETY, TUCSON

Chili Gravy

Wilma Turley of Sundown Ranch, Aripine, lived far enough from any market to learn how to make do and add flavor to leftovers. This gravy has so much character it could have made the first page of that classic cookbook, Granny Rowed A Gravy Boat.

Melt butter or drippings in iron fry pan. Add flour and stir until rich brown. Slowly stir in cold water and continue to stir as it cooks so it won't lump up. Taste and add salt, if needed. Brown meat with garlic and chili powder in a skillet, then add to the gravy, which should be contentedly bubbling. Simmer a few minutes, then serve over fresh, hot biscuits, mashed potatoes, or fluffy rice. Makes 5 or 6 rib-sticking servings.

1½ tablespoons butter or beef drippings
2 tablespoons flour
1 cup cold water
salt, if needed
2 to 3 cups meat, chopped, cubed, or ground
1 clove garlic, chopped or crushed
1 tablespoon red chili powder
hot biscuits, mashed potatoes, or rice

Biltmore Chili con Carne

The Arizona Biltmore Hotel was built in 1929, with its quarter-million concrete blocks cast in molds right on the property. Emry Kopta, artist and sculptor, designed the unique blocks, working with the architect, Charles MacArthur, a pupil of Frank Lloyd Wright. Crew members were the first to taste what was to become a standard, chili topped with a lime green cap of tongue-tingling guacamole.

Melt kidney fat in heavy kettle, then add meat and water. Cook 1 hour slowly; in fact, cook the whole batch slowly. Add onion; cook ½ hour. Stir in chili powder and cook another ½ hour. Add tomatoes; cook 1 hour, seasoning with paprika and more salt, if needed. Top chili with guacamole made by blending peeled avocados with finely diced hot peppers, onion, lime juice, and Tabasco. Serve with tamales and fresh, hot tortillas or crisp corn tortilla wedges.

¼ pound kidney fat, diced
1 pound lean beef, diced
2 cups water
1 small onion, chopped
3 tablespoons chili powder
1 cup solid pack tomatoes
½ tablespoon paprika
salt to taste
6 ripe avocados
3 small, hot chile peppers
1 ounce finely chopped onion
1 teaspoon Mexican lime juice
1 dash Tabasco sauce

Chapter 5

Breads: Corn, Yeast, Slap, and Sour

The family of breads, like the family of man, comes in infinite sizes, shapes and colors. Corn breads, yeast breads, sourdough, muffins, pan and fry breads, biscuits, and slap breads all found a home here. Not so long ago, bread making was routine in every Arizona kitchen and at most campfires.

Ages before that, in early Indian Arizona, mesquite beans were ground to make cakes to be stacked and "cooked" by desert heat in holes in the ground—our first flat bread, a pat or slap bread.

Corn was grown 4,000 years ago, native to the Southwest, giving form to another flat bread—the tortilla—also a kind of slap bread. Alone or with wheat flour, corn was used for a variety of baked, fried, stove top, or steamed breads, all plain and good.

Long before Francisco Vásquez de Coronado led his expedition through Arizona in 1540, the Hopi Indians were planting corn and making crisp wisps of piki and blue corn bread. Corn is the focal point of their culture and religion and equally sacred to the Navajo, who sprinkle cornmeal at dawn as a blessing prior to making the breakfast fry bread.

It took a heap of tasting before I realized that fry bread, squaw bread, Indian popovers, and sopapillas were so much the same that one recipe covered all of them.

Old recipes do not call for specific pan sizes. Cookie used what was available, extending to flat stones. Pan breads were most often made in an iron skillet, usually corn based. Fry bread, too, was skillet bubbled and soon became fancied up into doughnuts and fritters.

Yeast bread began with a potato until the yeast cake originated, later to go the way the liquid yeast jug did when dry yeast proved it could lift the dough.

Quick, sometimes called "lightnin'" breads, came in the mid-1800s when new leavenings like saleratus, baking soda, and baking powder were introduced. Happily embraced by mama, speedily baked shortcake, nut and banana bread, and soda biscuits took the place of the time-consuming practice grandma went through with yeast bread.

A town that never really existed as an entity, yet represents all that was real in the history of Arizona's early development, occupies a scenic desert site in the hills north of Phoenix. Pioneer Arizona was opened in 1965 as a "living history museum," portraying both rural and town lifestyles from the 1850s until statehood was achieved in 1912.

Some structures are truly historic; dismantled at their original Arizona sites, then moved to Pioneer Arizona for reconstruction and restoration. Others were modeled after buildings which existed in various parts of the territory. Costumed interpreters demonstrate crafts of yesteryear, and live animals add to the reality of the setting.

Major points of interest include: Whiskey Road-to-Ruin Saloon, originally from Gila Bend; the Opera House; a Carpenter Shop modeled after an 1880 Prescott enterprise; a Victorian house, built by cattleman John Marion Sears; Tin and Weaving shops; the "wattle and daub" Stage Stop; the Schoolhouse and Teacherage; the Ranch Complex, an 1870 structure from the Gordon Canyon area near Globe; Pioneer's Church, reconstructed from St. Paul's Methodist Episcopal Church in Globe; an 1880 Spring House and Root Cellar; and the Flying V Cabin, moved from the Young area. Rifle ports cut in the walls indicate its possible involvement in the notorious Pleasant Valley War of the last century.

Operated by a nonprofit organization, Pioneer Arizona is open Wednesdays through Sundays throughout most of the year. Demonstrations include cooking and baking the pioneer way.

Cornmeal

Corn is our native grain and, for a long time, was our principal grain. The old classics like corn pone and mush, johnnycake, and spoon bread are less used, yet the corn tortilla and the variations on a corn bread theme continue in popularity.

Frances Williamson of Chloride added grated carrots and honey to her stone-ground cornmeal to make a tender, less crumbly corn bread. Mildred Hooper, writer and photographer of Peoria, added green chiles, sharp cheese, and a small jar of chopped pimentos to her corn bread, calling it Fiesta Bread. Lucille Denison of Strawberry cut two cups of green chile strips to heat up the center of her corn bread. Babe Daley's mother had the most popular boardinghouse in Phoenix, and she combined cornmeal and corn into spoon bread.

In *Hopi Cookery*, written by Juanita Tiger Kavena, who was a home economist on the Hopi Reservation, there are 23 recipes using corn, first in Hopi agriculture. The ingenious women even make spoons from corn husks for visitors on dance and feast days.

Corn Tortillas

Lydia Trejo taught me how to make a corn tortilla. She said they are easy to make and have two faces. That is, like a crepe or a pancake, one side is not like the other. The front side, that thin layer which peels off, is called the "raspada." My corn tortillas fell apart. Hers were perfect, an exercise in experience. Masa Harina can be purchased at most Arizona grocery stores.

Mix Masa Harina and salt in a bowl. Melt lard in the boiling water. Stirring steadily, pour into bowl, until resulting dough is stiff. You can use a mixer, 2 or 3 minutes at medium speed. Scoop a lump of dough the size of an egg into the palm of one hand. Pat it round and thin to 5 inches in diameter. Or use rolling pin, putting dough between two pieces of plastic wrap. In the old days, damp muslin was used. Another option is the tortilla press, a hinged, metal gadget which works. Have griddle or comal hot and cook one minute per side until evenly light brown. Keep warm in a napkin if using at once. Wrap securely to freeze as they dry easily (but do not discard as they fry into corn chips or can be used in casseroles, broken). Yield: a dozen 6-inch corn tortillas.

2 cups Masa Harina
1 teaspoon salt
1 tablespoon fresh lard or shortening
2½ cups boiling water

Wheat Flour Tortillas

Wheat flour tortillas originated in the northern region of Mexico and the southwestern United States. The reason is simple: those areas grew wheat. Sonorans perfected the art of making wheat tortillas to the point of stretching them to twenty-four, even thirty inches, thin enough to be transparent. They were best cooked on large comals or even on top of old-fashioned wood ranges.

While getting my tortilla education, I was steered to Avondale, where Cruz Acevedo forsook her modern kitchen to bake wheat tortillas under a ramada in the back yard on an old wood-burning stove. Her husband, Joe, then city manager of Avondale, found the stove and built the shelter. That's how hard a man will work to get perfect homemade tortillas.

2 cups white (wheat) flour
2 tablespoons fresh lard
1 teaspoon salt
½ cup warm water

Sift flour and salt into a bowl. Pure lard gives the best texture and flavor and it should be creamed, or mixed by hand, to the consistency of face cream. No mixers. Tortillas are made by hand. Work flour and salt with lard and mix well. Add warm water to make a soft dough. Flour varies; you may need more water. Knead dough until springy in a bowl or on a board. Divide dough into balls about the size of small eggs. Cover and allow to rest 10 to 20 minutes (one of the secrets of tender tortillas).

Pat thin with hands or roll thin with rolling pin. Bake, ungreased, on both sides, until freckled with brown. Heat should be medium-hot, as for pancakes, not hot-hot. If tortillas puff up, press down lightly with a clean towel. Recipe makes about a dozen 6-to-7-inch tortillas. Store any that are not wolfed down in a plastic bag and refrigerate or freeze.

Piki Bread

Hopi heritage dictated that a Hopi girl must be skilled at the piki stone before marriage. She learned to grind the blue corn very fine. She grew to know just how thin the blue corn batter must be to ensure a bread thin as paper yet flexible enough to roll up like a scroll. She was taught how to take care of the piki stone, usually a family heirloom. The Hopis are most particular about their stones, which are flat and the size of a small griddle, and to make Piki Bread, should be slick as ice. Keeping it smooth may be done with cooked brains, or a spinal cord, or it may be greased with ground watermelon seeds, which have enough natural oil to season and slick a stone.

1 cup juniper ashes or chamisa ashes
1 bundle dried straw
1 cup boiling water
3 cups water
1 cup blue cornmeal

To make piki, strain 1 cup juniper ashes or chamisa ashes through a bundle of dried straw or tied broom straw into a pot containing a cup of boiling water. Stir and let cool. Pour 3 cups water into a heavy pot with the strained ash and bring to a boil. Add 1 cup blue cornmeal. Stir. This makes a thin gruel which can be spread on the hot griddle very quickly and smoothly with the palm of the hand. Putting the batter on is trick enough; peeling it off without burning the hand is the mark of a successful Hopi breadmaker. Piki is then rolled immediately. It may be eaten at once or stacked, roll by roll, and carefully stored in a dry place.

Until recently, before the traditional young woman could be accepted as a possible wife, she had to set a basket of her piki before the home of the bridegroom-to-be. If rejected, the wedding was off.

Skill at the piki stone is part of every Hopi woman's heritage. Piki bread, a paper-thin delicacy made from stone ground corn blended into a pancake-batter consistency, is spread on the hot stone with a swish of the hand. Piki bread remains a traditional food in modern times.
E.D. NEWCOMER COLLECTION,
ARIZONA HISTORICAL SOCIETY

Heritage Cornmeal Cakes

"Born in the territory of Arizona, I am a product of the West." So wrote Marguerite Noble when Random House published her first novel, Filaree. *The Payson author, historian, and champion of women as tamers of the West is known for her cooking and for a kitchen latchstring that is always out.*

"Cornmeal cakes are part of America's history. They helped to win the West," she said. *"The pioneer housewife found cornmeal available, and inexpensive, the cakes quick to prepare, delicious and nutritious. The modern cook, by enriching the cakes with bran, wheat germ, and sunflower seeds, adds extra nutrients with a satisfying crunchiness."* For sunrise breakfast:

1 cup yellow cornmeal
1 cup cold water
1 teaspoon salt, if desired
2 cups boiling water

Mix cornmeal, cold water, and salt, then add gradually to 2 cups water boiling in heavy saucepan. Cook 5 minutes. Remove from fire. Pour into greased loaf pan. Cover to prevent crust from forming. Chill until set. Slice into ¼-inch portions. Fry in buttered skillet, or use bacon drippings, just enough to keep mush from sticking.When golden brown on both sides, serve warm with butter and syrup, honey, or molasses. Or you may prefer homemade jelly: prickly pear, wild grape, or algerita berry. One loaf serves 4 or 5. If desired, add to mush while cooking: 2 tablespoons each, wheat germ, unprocessed bran, and sunflower seeds.

Hardtack

Although hardtack is thought of as ship's biscuit, it was used by many pioneers and the United States Army because of its ability to keep over long periods. One food historian, Florence Ekstrand, wrote about Scandinavians who started west with a whole barrel of what they called "flatbrod." The Army had better names for it: sheet iron, teeth dullers, and artillery. The *Old West Army Cook Book* gave this recipe.

"Mix 4 cups of flour and 4 teaspoons salt with enough water to make a dough stiff enough to roll out or pat out ½-inch thick. Cut into squares about 3 by 3 inches. Use a nail and punch 4 rows of 4 holes each on both sides. Bake on an ungreased pan for 30 minutes at 375 degrees. Turn and bake another 30 minutes." Ten pieces of fried brick.

Salt Rising Bread

This old fashioned bread which combined cornmeal and flour was no mystery to Mrs. R. B. Wooley of Houserock Valley Ranch at Jacob Lake.

Scald the sweet milk. Add cornmeal and a teaspoon of sugar. Set in warm place overnight: 100 degrees is about right. (That's warm.) Cover well. In the morning, add salt, a tablespoon of sugar, and lukewarm water with enough flour to make a stiff batter, beginning with 3 cups. Beat thoroughly until smooth. Keep warm until dough rises, than add melted fat and more flour so that dough is again stiff. Knead well until satiny. Divide into 2 loaves and place in greased bread pans. Set in warm place until they rise double. Bake about 45 minutes at 350 degrees—with wood stove, moderate oven, increasing heat in any oven the last 20 minutes to 375-400 degrees. Let bread cool very slowly, by wrapping loaves in clean towels.

1 pint sweet milk
4 heaping tablespoons cornmeal
1 teaspoon sugar
1 teaspoon salt
1 tablespoon sugar
1 quart lukewarm water
flour to make stiff batter
2 tablespoons fat, melted

Chile Corn Bread

Babe Daley's mother ran a boardinghouse in old Phoenix, serving such good food that the town's leading physician, Dr. Payne Palmer, came in for a meal whenever he could take time. This is Babe's adaptation of her mother's spoon bread.

Mix together the cornmeal, soda, buttermilk, salt, corn oil, and eggs. Pour half into a buttered 2-quart casserole alternately with chiles and two-thirds of the cheese. Top with remaining batter and cheese. Bake at 350 degrees 45-50 minues or until a knife inserted in the center comes out clean. Babe's husband Frank says it goes better with ham or fried chicken than dessert.

1 cup cornmeal
1 pinch baking soda
¾ cup buttermilk
½ teaspoon salt
1 can (16-ounce) creamed corn
⅓ cup corn oil
2 eggs, lightly beaten
1 can (4-ounce) diced green chiles, drained
1 cup grated sharp cheese

Bakery Rhyme

Breathes there a wife with soul so dead
Who never to her husband has said:
"This is my own, real homemade bread."?

This grain-enriched verse began the baking section of the first cookbook compiled by the Pink Ladies of the Good Samaritan Hospital Auxiliary of Phoenix.

Yeast

The first yeast used to lift a dough of flour and water was fermented beer—and the Greeks did it.

"Two quarts of water, in which a cup of hops have been boiled; four potatoes, boiled and mashed; a cup of sugar and a half cup of salt. (Less of sugar and salt may be used in cold weather as these are designed to arrest excessive fermentation.) Mix well, allowing time to rise and then bottle for use. Some add flour for thickening, but it will keep longer without it. It should always be kept a few days to rise, or some old yeast (a cupful) may be used to raise it before bottling."

Excerpt from an old cookbook, dated 1872, assembled by the Ladies Aid of the First Lutheran Church, Fry (now Sierra Vista).

2 quarts water, boiled
1 cup hops
4 potatoes
1 cup sugar
½ cup of salt

Sourdough

Sourdough legends are impressive if difficult to substantiate. It is said Columbus brought sourdough with him.

Western folklore reports that in some families, sourdough starter was handed down from generation to generation. The starter was really the yeast that made the bread rise with distinctive flavor and most old-timers had a recipe for starter. Some used a potato, some used sugar, some just the wild yeast in the air—some put together all three ingredients.

Stella Hughes, author and food historian, wrote me about ranch cooking: "Bread was, and is, cooked at every meal. The roundup cook preferred sourdough starter and the loss of his starter was classified as a major calamity. Not that starters were so hard to make. It took from three to five days for a new starter to become active enough to use. Virtually every meal drew on the starter for bread, biscuits, pancakes, even cookies and cakes.

"Sourdough was kept in a keg or crock, never in metal. Each day the cook replaced the necessary proportions of flour and water and set the starter in a warm place to ferment, even taking the well-wrapped keg to bed on cold nights.

"Almost all old-time cooks mixed their dough in a dishpan of flour but some mixed their dough right in the top of the flour sack. Making a well in the middle of the flour, they'd pour in the starter, water, sugar and salt, and begin mixing by turning in small handfuls of flour. It was worked until smooth, then biscuits were pinched off to put in, usually, the Dutch oven. No mixing bowl, no breadboard, no rolling pin; simple."

Art Perry's Sourdough

Art Perry was born in Flagstaff, could carve a willow whistle and do bird calls, and knew the best of outdoor cooking secrets, starting with sourdough. His sourdough starter went all ways. Beat in a couple of eggs and you've got everyday pancakes. Add sweet corn cut off the cob to make corn oysters. Add a little sugar, milk, and soda and the result is fancy Sunday pancakes.

To make sourdough starter, use only a glass, pottery, stone, plastic, or wooden utensil. No metal. Stir yeast and sugar together with a little water to make a smooth paste. Add raw potato, the rest of the water, and flour to thicken. Beat well, then cover with a clean towel, and let set a few days until the mixture is good and sour and bubbly.

When it smells good, feed the bubbles 1 cup of flour or whatever amount it takes to make elastic, smooth dough, not sticky. Always start sourdough bread, rolls, or pancakes with sourdough starter at room temperature. And always save 1 cup of starter from each batch (or by feeding starter regularly) in order to have starter on hand for another time. A good feeding is 1 cup flour, ½ cup water, and 1 teaspoon sugar to a batch of starter at room temperature. It will begin to bubble about 2 hours after being fed. Use it when it bubbles.

1 package dry yeast
2 tablespoons sugar
1 pint water
1 large raw potato, peeled and quartered
4 cups flour

Jean Hazlewood's Sourdough Biscuits

Jean Hazlewood powered husband Earl, three children, all hired hands, and a couple of mean-looking, tender-hearted dogs with the biggest sourdough biscuits I ever saw. They were a regular part of breakfast at dawn and went along to lunch. "Cowboys can get ulcers, one of the unromantic things the public doesn't know," Jean said. "They leave at 5 a.m. and stay out all day. They ignore hunger, so the stomach juices over-produce. Biscuits and jerky can be preventive medicine, carried as a snack."

Sift dry ingredients together. Cut in butter or stir in oil and add sourdough starter. Mix well. Turn dough out on lightly floured board. Knead until shiny. Roll out ½ inch thick. Cut with floured 3-inch cutter. Place biscuits in well-greased baking pan. Brush with melted butter. Let rise in warm spot 1 hour. Bake 20 minutes at 425 degrees. Makes 12 big biscuits.

1½ cups flour
2 teaspoons baking powder
½ teaspoon baking soda
1 scant teaspoon salt
¼ cup butter or cooking oil
1 cup sourdough starter

Casa Vieja Roman Bread

La Casa Vieja has been a part of Tempe history for years—long before Arizona State University evolved from Tempe Normal and began winning national athletic titles. In 1871, Charles Trumbull Hayden built a gracious adobe home on the banks of the Salt River which offered welcome hospitality to weary travelers. Now converted to a restaurant, the Casa's traditional Roman Bread is still served, made with flour from nearby Hayden Flour Mills.

Combine sugar, yeast, and lukewarm water, stirring to dissolve yeast. Stir in the flour, a cup at a time, then add 1½ teaspoons of salt and the onion. Mix well, then knead on lightly floured board until smooth. Place dough in an oiled bowl and let rise until doubled, covered with a clean linen towel. When doubled, punch down again. Flatten out dough on an oiled cookie sheet. When an even 1 inch thick across, pat the top of the dough lightly with corn oil. Let dough rise again until doubled. Sprinkle with remaining salt and the rosemary. Bake in oven, preheated to 400 degrees, for 20 to 25 minutes. Serve hot.

1 tablespoon sugar
1 cake yeast
1½ cups lukewarm water
4 cups Hayden Flour Mills Family Kitchen flour (or any all-purpose flour)
2 teaspoons salt, divided
½ cup finely chopped onion
2 tablespoons dried rosemary, finely crushed
2 teaspoons corn oil

Cornish Bread Buns

In 1900, Bisbee was a small mining town in the Arizona Territory, still fearful of the fierce Apaches. Even so, the wealth of the mines attracted Canadians, English, Irish, and Scots, most of whom brought wives unprepared for the likes of Brewery Gulch. The Bisbee Woman's Club was formed and bazaars and parties funded the treasury. As always when women meet, the exchange of recipes added to the pleasure of planning a library, a clubhouse, or a kindergarten. Cornish Bread Buns survived from that day to appear again in the Bicentennial Cookbook.

Let scalded milk cool to lukewarm, then add butter, sugar, and salt. Dissolve yeast cake (or use 1 package dry yeast) in lukewarm water. Combine cooled milk mixture and yeast liquid to 3 cups of flour. Beat thoroughly. Cover and let rise until light. Turn out of pan and knead in about 2 cups of flour, or more if necessary to make a smooth, elastic dough. Let rise until doubled. Knead again on floured board and roll out ⅓ inch thick. Cut buns with small biscuit cutter, brush tops with melted butter and place in greased pans. Let rise until doubled in bulk, then bake about 15 minutes or until brown, in 425-degree oven. Amount will fill three square 8 by 8 by 2-inch pans, or make 27 Cornish buns.

2 cups scalded milk
3 tablespoons butter
2 tablespoons sugar
2 tablespoons salt
1 yeast cake
¼ cup lukewarm water
5 to 6 cups flour

Old-Fashioned Vinegar Rolls

This old standby recipe came from LaVerne Logreen, whose father, Bert Davis, was the first white child born in Pine, Arizona. The doctor promptly tucked all three pounds of him into a man's hat.

In a small saucepan combine vinegar, water, 1 cup sugar, and 2 teaspoons of cinnamon. Stir over low heat until sugar dissolves. Cook over medium heat 20 minutes to make a syrup. Set aside. Mix and sift flour, baking powder, and salt. Cut in shortening, which was once called fresh lard or home-churned butter, but now is more often known as Crisco. Stir milk in, using fork, until a soft dough forms. Lightly flour the board and roll dough out into a rectangle ¼ inch thick. Sprinkle remaining sugar and cinnamon over surface. Dot with two tablespoons butter. Roll up from longer side. Cut crosswise slices a generous 1 inch thick. Place cut side up, close together, in deep baking dish. Dot with remaining butter. Pour over all the hot vinegar mix. Bake 30 to 40 minutes at 375 degrees. Serve hot with heavy pouring cream. Serves 8.

¾ cup cider vinegar
1½ cups water
1¼ cups sugar, divided
4 teaspoons cinnamon, divided
2 cups sifted, enriched flour
1 tablespoon baking powder
1 teaspoon salt
⅓ cup shortening
¾ cup milk
4 tablespoons butter

Nel's Potato Bread

Nel Sweeten came to visit a cousin, Delia Gist, in 1922, and fell in love with Arizona and a dashing young rancher, Roy Cooper. They married, had three sons and built the state's largest goat ranch. When Roy was tragically killed, Nel converted the ranch to cattle. In 1970, the Hassayampa River swept her home and all her possessions away. Undaunted, she began again at age 72, adding a career in writing.

In 1985, she was inducted into the National Cowgirl Hall of Fame. She wrote the introduction to the "Bread" chapter of their 1983 Arizona State Cowbelles Cookbook, *and included her delightful, informal recipe for potato bread, which she said liberated her forever from biscuits.*

Peel potato and slice; cook in 1 quart water. When tender, mash potato in a large bowl with a little of the potato water, reserving the balance of the water to use as bread liquid when it has cooled to lukewarm. Mix in all other ingredients, adding flour and other water gradually. (Nel preferred bacon drippings for shortening and used it liberally on her hands as she worked the dough.) Work into a smooth sponge; set aside in a warm place to double in bulk. Then punch down and really knead, working away any grudges. ("You'll feel better and your bread will be lighter," she added.) Let rise again. When double, punch down again and form into 5 or 6 medium loaves, or 3 dozen big rolls. Bake at 350 degrees— 45 minutes for bread; 20 minutes for rolls.

1 potato, fist size
1 cup bacon drippings
2 cups sugar
6 cups water, including potato water
2 packages dry yeast
14 cups flour
1 tablespoon salt

Bolillos

These crunchy, flavorful hard rolls won quick acceptance during the brief, ill-fated reign of Maximilian and Carlotta, appointed by Napoleon III to impose French rule on Mexico. French rule went; the French roll stayed. The Bolillo became one of the stars of the panadería *(the bakery). Just as the French shop each day for fresh bread, the Mexican cook prefers to select dinner Bolillos at the bakery, where shelves or windows offer tempting sizes and shapes of* pan dulce *(sweet breads). In Arizona, every mining town and border community has an enticing little bakeshop, Bolillos going out the door as fast as they emerge from the oven.*

1 package active dry yeast
3 teaspoons sugar
1 teaspoon salt
2 cups warm water
2 tablespoons warm butter
6 cups unbleached, hard wheat flour
2 tablespoons fresh lard or shortening
1 teaspoon cornstarch
½ cup water

Stir yeast, sugar, and salt together, then dissolve in warm water. As mixture bubbles, add butter, then add flour, 2 cups at a time until the fifth cup, beating well at each addition. Add flour slowly after the fifth cup, stopping when dough gets too stiff to mix. Use remaining flour to dust board and hands, then begin kneading until dough is elastic and satiny. Place in large, well-greased bowl. Turn once to grease top. Cover with clean towel, and let rise in warm place free of drafts. Dough will double in 1 to 1½ hours. Punch down, cover and let rise again. Now the fun part.

Form into long cylinders, or ropes, about 2 inches in diameter. Cup or snip off 3-inch pieces of dough, twisting each end. Bolillos have a distinctive, shuttle shape and are always gashed on top. Place rolls about 2 inches apart on lightly floured baking sheets. Gash tops with floured knife. Cover with clean towels, again allowing to double. To make extra crusty, dissolve the cornstarch in the water and bring to a boil, stirring. Allow to cool, then brush tops thinly as oven heats to 400 degrees. Bake 30 to 40 minutes until color is a lightly tanned blush. Best served at once, like tortillas, with lots of butter. To keep, let them cool before wrapping, airtight. Yield: 3 dozen, more or less, probably more.

Ruth's Whole Wheat Yeast Rolls

Ruth Bennett was always implored to bake her rolls when her husband, Bones Bennett, barbecued in his mesquite-fired, volcano-rock-lined pit. The Glendale couple cooked for crowds, causing Ruth to say, matter-of-factly, "I've baked these rolls as often as four times a day."

Dissolve yeast in warm water in large bowl. To scald milk, heat just to boiling point. Stir in shortening, salt, and brown sugar or honey. Cool. Add yeast-water mixture and eggs, stirring well. Gradually add flour, a cup at a time. (Half whole-grain white flour may be used with the wheat, if preferred.) When dough leaves the sides of the bowl, knead on floured board 10 to 15 minutes. Let rise about 1 hour in the bowl. Knead again 5 minutes. Shape into rolls and place in baking pans to rise until double in bulk. Bake at 350 degrees for 25 minutes. Makes 2 dozen rolls.

1 yeast cake
¼ cup warm water
1 cup milk, scalded
½ cup shortening or oil
1 ½ teaspoons salt
½ cup (scant) brown sugar or honey
2 small eggs
4 ½ cups whole wheat flour

Hilda's Yeast Dough

Hilda Baer of Mesa learned to cook as a child in Russia. When an older sister brought her to New York, she baked her way into their hearts. Another move, to Arizona, meant another triumph. She got out her rolling pin and baked herself a new batch of friends. This dough is her basic for coffee cake, rolls, cheese buns, or cinnamon roll. They sold for seven dollars up at Temple Beth Sholom during building fund days.

Empty yeast into small bowl. Using paper envelope which held yeast, twice fill with lukewarm water and sprinkle on yeast, a little more than 2 tablespoons. Add sugar. Set aside in warm place to rise. Into large bowl, sift 4 cups flour. After yeast has risen to fill small bowl, pour mixture into large bowl with flour, salt, sugar, and the 3 whole eggs. Cut in butter, oleo, or favorite shortening. Have sour cream and milk at room temperature. Add to mixture; mix and knead well until soft and silky. Put in warm place until double in bulk. In the winter, Mrs. Baer makes it at night and lets it rise until morning. Otherwise, she covers it with clean cloth and sets in the sun. It is not necessary to reknead the dough. Form rolls, coffee cake, or buns and allow to double. Then bake at 350 degrees until golden brown.

1 envelope dry yeast
lukewarm water
2 tablespoons sugar
4 to 5 cups flour
½ teaspoon salt
1 cup sugar
3 eggs, whole
¼ pound shortening
½ cup commercial sour cream
½ cup milk

Fry Bread

Ah, fry bread. An instant hit from the moment I burned my fingers and honeyed my lip at the first Phoenix Indian School Open House I attended. My favorite fry bread story came from marvelous Anna Kopta, who taught Indian children for fifty years and married Emry Kopta, distinguished sculptor whose work lives on in the Smithsonian and Heard Museum.

He once traveled on a lengthy sheep-buying trip with Lorenzo Hubbell, whose trading post at Ganado on the Navajo Reservation is now a National Historic Site. Kopta received the name *Dah-de-nill-yaz*, Navajo for fry bread, because of the amount of it he ate. Hubbell carried along a jar of butter mixed with Roquefort cheese to spread on his bread. When the Navajos smelled the cheese, he was offered a sweat bath for instant purification. "That food has been dead too long," they said.

Cowbelle Fry Bread

In The Chuck Box, *a cookbook put together by Northern Arizona Cowbelles, a homey recipe was submitted for Navajo Fry Bread by Lena Aja. This is the basic method used by campers, Boy and Girl Scouts, ranch cooks, and this writer.*

Measure dry ingredients into deep mixing bowl. Add shortening and knead with hands until dough is in small pea-size pieces. Add warm, not hot, water and knead with hands until dough is smooth and leaves sides of bowl. Knead at least 5 minutes. Cover with clean dish towel, place in warm place to rise for 30 minutes. The secret, according to Lena, for tender, light Fry Bread, is in the kneading and resting, but she said, boys usually start frying after 10 minutes. Divide dough into portions about golf-ball size and pat, slap, or roll out as round as possible, ¼ inch thick. Fry in hot shortening or oil about 1 inch in depth. Fry both sides until light golden, not dark brown. Top with refried beans, powdered sugar, or honey.

A Navajo Taco is Fry Bread of generous proportions, heaped with beans, grated cheese, chopped lettuce, tomato, and onion, and jolts of fired-up salsa.

3 cups flour
3 teaspoons baking powder
1 tablespoon shortening, lard, or corn oil
1 teaspoon salt
¾ cup warm water

A Prescott-area ranch wife performs one of her regular kitchen chores, kneading bread dough. Now a rarity in American kitchens, bread-baking was a necessity in 1915, when she was photographed.
SHARLOT HALL MUSEUM

Kneeldown Bread

Annie Dodge Wauneka, daughter of the great Navajo leader, Chee Dodge, won the Medal of Freedom for organizing the fight against diseases that killed her people, particularly tuberculosis. Even so, Annie was expected to do and did the traditional chores of Navajo women. They take full charge of the home and the sheep and do the butchering and cooking, which means making many interesting breads in addition to the morning Fry Bread. Kneeldown Bread is a tasty example.

Scrape the kernels from fresh corn and grind on a metate. Make small packages of the resulting mush by wrapping small portions in cornhusks, using several layers of husk. Put the packages in hot ashes. Cover with fresh husks or leaves and slightly moist dirt, then with hot coals. Build a small, quick fire over Kneeldown Bread and bake at least 1 hour. Remove packages from fire, peel off husks, and eat while hot. Navajo tamales!

To meet John Lorenzo Hubbell's needs, thirty to forty loaves of bread were baked daily. Some were eaten by his family, and the rest were sold to Navajos who lived in the area around Hubbell's Trading Post.
NATIONAL PARK SERVICE.

Beaten Biscuits

An early settler in Tubac brought this sanctified southern belle recipe with her from Virginia. Knowing there undoubtedly is not one cook today who will beat biscuit dough, I nevertheless transcribe this just as a member of the Tubac Museum gave it to me, for historical purposes.

One tablespoon of sugar in one quart of flour. One good tablespoon of lard. One-fourth teaspoonful of soda, not over ½ teaspoonful of baking powder, 1 teaspoonful of salt. Mix thoroughly and add ½ cupful of cold water with ½ cup sweet milk off ice. Knead well, then beat 20 or 30 minutes with a heavy mallet. To have good success, the dough should be smooth and blistered. Cut with cutter 1½ inches in diameter. Print top with fork. Bake 35 minutes until light brown in medium oven.

1 tablespoon sugar
1 quart flour
1 tablespoon lard
¼ teaspoon soda
½ teaspoon baking powder
1 teaspoon of salt
½ cup cold water
½ cup sweet milk

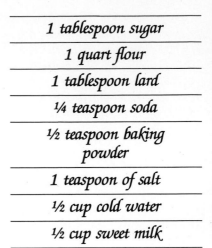

Lela Cartwright Hon's Biscuits

Reddick J. Cartwright led about a dozen families west from Illinois, following the Union Pacific railroad tracks so the wagon train couldn't wander off course. Eventually, members of the Cartwright family homesteaded hundreds of acres near Seven Springs and in West Phoenix. They got together often for reunions. Lela Cartwright Hon was always asked to bring her high, bronzed biscuits. To her embarrassment, at one dinner it was impossible to sink a tooth into those usually flaky rounds.

The family teased her unmercifully about her lead sinkers. One biscuit was saved and, at every occasion thereafter, that biscuit appeared. Some wag even had it epoxied, and it became known as Lela's Traveling Biscuit. This recipe is not Lela's Traveling Biscuit, these biscuits will melt in your mouth.

Sift flour, baking powder, soda, and salt into a big mixing bowl. Lightly flour hands and work shortening and butter into mixture. Add buttermilk and stir in with fork. When dough is gathered and leaves the side of the bowl, pat out on floured board or other flat surface, and cut with a floured biscuit cutter. (Dough should be no more than ½ inch thick.) Place on greased cookie sheet. Have hot oven ready, about 450 degrees. Bake each pan of biscuits about 12 minutes. Makes 28 to 30 light, but rich biscuits.

3 cups flour
5 teaspoons baking powder
1 teaspoon baking soda
1½ teaspoons salt
2 heaping tablespoons Crisco or fresh lard
1 heaping tablespoon butter
1¼ cups buttermilk

(RIGHT) The "fort" at Pipe Spring protected early settlers against Indian raiders. But it was also home. The dining corner has been preserved at Pipe Spring National Monument, much as it was when the settlement was built.
NATIONAL PARK SERVICE

Grandmother Stewart's
Raisin Biscuits

Jack Stewart's Camelback Inn, now owned by the Marriott Hotel Corporation, operated more than thirty years with a firm policy on cuisine: Just Good Plain American Food. They fixed carrots six ways, but there was only one way to make Raisin Biscuits. That was his mother's Scotch-Canadian way.

Sift the first four ingredients into a bowl. With hands, mix in butter. Add raisins, milk, and cream. When dough forms a ball and leaves sides of bowl, pat out lightly on floured board to about ⅓-inch thickness. Cut with lightly floured 2-inch biscuit cutter. If you like crustier biscuits, roll out thinner. Bake 10 to 15 minutes on ungreased baking sheet in 425-degree oven. Recipe makes 3 dozen rich, flaky, tender biscuits.

4 cups sifted flour
8 teaspoons baking powder
1 teaspoon salt
1 cup sugar
1 cup butter, warm
2 cups raisins
¾ cup milk
1 cup cream

Bessie's Beefy Muffins

Horace B. Hall Jr. swept his wife into marriage after three months courtship. Blonde, dimpled Bessie became the mother of six, helped Horace milk fifty cows twice a day, and tried a new beef dish whenever company came to Laveen. What she did with the leftovers is a wonderfully sneaky way to stretch a little meat into a hearty meal.

Grind leftover roast beef, trimmed of any fat and bone. Moisten with chopped onion. Add a very little beef broth, seasoning with salt and pepper, if needed. Make a rich biscuit dough to which add 1 cup of cornmeal. Line muffin pans with dough. Fill with beef mixture. Top with more dough. Bake about 20 minutes at 400 degrees. Just right with cowboy beans, a green salad, and for the Halls, milk, of course.

leftover roast beef
chopped onion
beef broth
seasoning, salt & pepper to taste
biscuit dough
1 cup cornmeal

Hearty Mesquite Muffins

Desert food cooking classes are held at both the Desert Botanical Garden in Phoenix and the Tucson Botanical Garden, emphasizing the use of nature's groceries. The uninteresting look of a mesquite pod puts off the unknowing. But a few bites of mesquite bean muffins with mesquite jelly brings a turnaround.

To make mesquite bean-pod flour, fully ripe beans with no beetle holes must be picked from trees on the desert floor. Clean beans and heat in a 170-degree oven 4 hours to destroy any internal troublemakers. Or sun dry as the Indians do. Grinding is work if you do it the ethnic way and use a mortar or two stones. A food processor or blender crushes just fine. Sift seed coats and fiber from meal, then sift again for a finer flour, golden and sweet. Not white. Mesquite has a natural sweetening with peanut butter-like flavor which Indian children love. You may substitute wheat flour for no more than half the mesquite flour in the recipe.

Mix flours. Combine egg, salad oil, and milk, and whip with a fork until frothy. Add liquid mixture to dry flours and stir just until moistened. Fill one dozen well-greased muffin cups with batter, ⅔ full. Bake 25 minutes at 400 degrees. Cool slightly to remove. Try the recipe once without spice to taste the true flavor of mesquite flour, but add cinnamon or nutmeg to another batch, if desired. These muffins are dubbed hearty because of their rich, moist crumb.

⅔ cup mesquite flour
1⅓ cups sifted self-rising flour
1 beaten egg
¼ cup salad oil
¾ cup milk

Tillie Luke's Popovers

Tillie Luke was the mother of Frank Luke Jr., Arizona's heroic aviator of World War I for whom Luke Air Force Base was named. His favorite treat was a triple delight: hot popovers with homemade butter and home-cooked jam.

Mix flour and salt in bowl. Beat eggs until light. Add to flour, alternating with milk into which sugar should be stirred. Mix well but do not overbeat. Have oven heated to 450 degrees. Fill buttered custard cups or hissing hot gem pans ⅓ full only. Do not overload. Bake 20 minutes, then lower heat to 350 degrees without peeping. Bake 15 to 20 minutes more. If not cooked long enough, popovers collapse. Yield: 10 popovers.

1¼ cups flour
¼ teaspoon salt
2 eggs
1 teaspoon sugar
1 cup milk
butter

Wonderful Date-Nut Bread

Any recipe that begins with putting the kettle on to boil has more than a hint of heritage. This was a specialty of Mrs. Marie Stalnaker, one of the first presidents of the Arizona Federation of Garden Clubs, Inc.

Fill kettle with water and put on to boil. Set oven at 350 degrees. Grease 4 small (3 by 5-inch) loaf pans and flour lightly and evenly. Cut dates in half. Break nuts, but not too small. Pour 2 cups boiling water over the date and nut pieces and let stand while mixing the batter. Cream the shortening in a bowl, adding brown sugar gradually. Sift flour and salt together twice.

Break eggs, 1 at a time, into the shortening mixture, hand beating after each addition. Add baking soda to dates and nuts. Stir flour and fruit mixture alternately into creamed batter. Stir gently; mix quickly. Now stir in another ⅔ cup water and fold in. Pour into pans and bake 45 minutes or until toothpick tested in center comes out clean and dry. Turn out of pans to cool. Better tomorrow and wonderful next week.

water
shortening
flour
4 cups cut-up dates
2 cups broken nuts
2 cups boiling water
½ cup shortening
1½ cups brown sugar, firmly packed
4 cups sifted cake flour
1 teaspoon salt
2 eggs
2 teaspoons baking soda
⅔ cup hot water

Shovel Flapjacks

In the Old South, where most plantation workers had few utensils, it was said they washed the hoe and baked a few corncakes over the fire, calling them hoecakes. Sue Cavness McDaniel gave this related recipe for shovel cakes to Bonnie Peplow when she was putting together the range cookbook, Roundup Recipes. *Bonnie said she thought it was the most interesting recipe in the book.*

"One year on the trail to Bitter Creek, Papa made what he called Shovel Flapjacks. We had one pack horse and, of course, were traveling light. We had no Dutch oven but had a short-handled shovel with us. Hence the flapjacks' name."

"This makes a stiff dough. Use your hands to mold a piece of dough about 6 inches in diameter and 1 inch thick. Put this flapjack on the clean shovel which has been heating on hot coals dragged from the campfire. Allow to brown on one side. Then turn and cook on the other side. Of course, we could carry no butter but broke the flapjacks into small pieces and dipped them in the syrup, which is a standby on any ranch."

2 cups flour
1 teaspoon salt
3 teaspoons baking powder
4 tablespoons bacon drippings or other fat
⅔ cup water or milk
syrup

Pumpkin Johnnycake

The best prescription written out by Dr. Ward R. Gillespie of mountainous Greer was for this surprising johnnycake.

Mix until smooth and silky and bake in greased 9 by 12 pan about 30 minutes in 350-degree oven.

1 cup pumpkin
1 cup black molasses
1 cup flour
1 cup cornmeal
1 cup sour milk
1 teaspoon soda
1 egg
pinch of salt

Pancakes Common

With nearly half a pound of flour, mix five well-beaten eggs, and then add, by degrees, a quart of good milk; fry them in fresh lard, and serve them with pounded loaf sugar strewn between each, or with Mashed Apple Filling made by cutting apples very small and stewing them with a little white wine, brown sugar, grated lemon peel and pounded cinnamon. Mash smooth to spread over pancakes. Roll them up and sprinkle with sifted loaf-sugar.

From *The Cook's Oracle* of 1822

Grandmother's Pancakes

Pancakes are an American passion, and all varieties could be found in Arizona. Most of them were beaten together with eggs, except for cornmeal johnnycakes. Hoecakes, griddle cakes, flapjacks, a string of flats, flannel cakes, and buckwheat cakes appeared on both breakfast and supper tables in puddles of molasses, maple syrup, cane syrup, or brown sugar. With sausage cakes, of course, and a fried egg on top of the stack. Cattlemen took their pancakes with steak; hog farmers liked theirs with bacon or ham. Alice Phillips of Phoenix, who had Vermont roots, preferred hers exactly the way her grandmother made them.

1½ cups flour
1½ teaspoons baking powder
3 tablespoons sugar
1 teaspoon salt
4 eggs
3 tablespoons melted butter
milk

Sift together the flour, sugar, salt, and baking powder in a mixing bowl. Add the eggs, melted butter, and enough milk to make a batter. Simply blend together; do not beat or otherwise try to smooth the mixture. The lumps are all right. Batter has enough milk when it pours easily off the spoon into the pan and smooths out. Makes cakes 8 inches in diameter, not the dainty dabs so commonly seen. Use a big iron skillet. When bubbles appear on top of pancake, turn and fry the other side. The butter should keep them from sticking but Alice preferred them fried in hot fat. She also insisted they must be served with pure Vermont syrup.

Chapter 6
Meats: Tame and Game

Game came with the territory in Arizona and, like our widely varied landscape, ranges from desert animals to the elk, or wapiti, and the mountain bighorn sheep.

There are nine species of big game: antelope, mule deer, whitetail deer, elk, mountain bighorn sheep, black bear, mountain lion, javelina, and bison, which is not native but was brought in.

The natural inhabitants of the state ate most of the natural game of the territory, cooked and uncooked. H. Thomas Cain, who came to Arizona as curator of the prestigious Heard Museum, told me, "It took man a million years to learn to cook his meat. Now that we have learned, I prefer mine well done." As an anthropologist, he tried beaver tail and moose nose without pleasure, but the Indian learned to enjoy what was available.

When Father Kino introduced the cow and the lamb to this region in 1687, they were accepted almost too enthusiastically. The great Spanish haciendas that flourished from 1790 to 1820 were finally abandoned due to persistent attacks by Apaches. They preferred beef steak to bear steak and, except for the Presidio of Tubac, steadily raided the ranchers. Pimas, deadly enemies of the Apaches, were trained and stationed at Tubac, but this protection vanished when the garrison was moved to Tucson.

One intrepid family, which inherited Don Toribio de Otero's Spanish grant of 1789, came to be among the most successful cattle ranchers in the territory. During the Civil War, when protection was gone, they moved to Sonora, Mexico, but came back. *The Arizona Star* of October 10, 1884, stated: "Sabino Otero last week sold 12,000 head of cattle for $35,000 . . . steers in prime condition." He built a fine home in Tucson, went to Europe, joined the Arizona Pioneers Historical Society in 1889, and ran cattle "on a thousand hills."

In the sagas of Colin and Cameron and Hooker, Hooper, and Hines, it is sometimes forgotten that Mexican ranchers are the oldest in the business.

Drought succeeded the Apache as a deterrent to cattle ranching, but the railroads and rain kept the rancher in business. In the 1890s, a good cowboy earned $30 a month. Prime beef sold for eight to ten cents a pound. Individual ranches became fenced, range branding disappeared, and new enemies continued to challenge the cattle and sheep grower. The developer and the medical attack on meat are the current foes. The wives of growers organized into national groups to protect their lifestyle and educate the public.

As a food historian, my statement is, "Meat won the West." I'm not sure vegetarians could have done it.

William Sherley Williams was one of the fearless breed of men who roamed the mountainous West before better-known explorers opened the vastness for cattlemen, miners, railroads, and emigrants. His passing through Northern Arizona became a matter of permanent record by the naming for him of a river, a mountain, and a town.

Later, Bill Williams received a different sort of fame from a group of latter-day mountain men. Like most small towns, Williams sometimes felt an identity crisis, and in 1953, a group of residents conceived the idea of promoting their town through appearances by buckskin-clad "mountain men" replicating the fearless breed of years past.

Their first out-of-town appearance was in the 1953 Phoenix Rodeo Parade. Determined to do more than just look the part, they rode the 180 miles from Williams to Phoenix, camping along the way.

To date, Bill Williams Mountain Men have won more than 200 trophies for parades and other appearances, and have whooped it up in four presidential inauguration parades in Washington, D.C.

Roast Beef

Beef Ala Mode. Take a rump or piece of beef, bone it, beat it well, and lard it with fat bacon, then put it into a stewpan with some rind of bacon, a calf's foot, an onion, carrot, a bunch of sweet herbs, a bay leaf, thyme, a clove of garlic, some cloves, salt and pepper, pour over the whole a glass of water, let it stew over a slow fire for six hours at least. A clean cloth should be placed over the stewpan before the lid is put on, which must be carefully closed. When it is done, strain the gravy through a sieve, clear off the fat, and serve.

From *The Cook's Own Book*, published in 1832
Brought to Phoenix by Myrtle Barnes.

Traditional roast beef, the dish of choice on Sunday, was done in a roaster with liquid added and often nestled with potatoes and vegetables. The Christmas roast was as large as possible and often, because of a strong early influence from the English who settled in Arizona, came with Yorkshire pudding. Nobody described the roast beef occasion better than Alberta Wilson Conant, whose *They Set A Good Table* was included in the *Southwest Review's* book, *Son-Of-A-Gun Stew.*

"The roast was put on the table in front of Papa along with the gravy. He carved with the speed and the precision of a surgeon. He had to or he would never have got anything to eat for himself. We were eight and waited rather patiently because we had had oyster stew from the blue and white tureen. Mama said at Grandmother's the recipe began: 'Take 100 oysters.' And the blessing was always short. Papa said the Lord meant hot food to be eaten hot. There were mashed potatoes as background for the gravy. Mattie passed the vegetables and then refilled the bowls for seconds and thirds . . . Nowadays they write articles about how to get your children to eat. Our worry was how to keep them from eating."

Barney Beef

The supermarket of today lacks versatility when compared with Hancock's Store, the first business establishment on the Phoenix Townsite in 1871. It served as store, courthouse, justice's office, and butcher shop. James Barney, historian, reported the proprietor killed a beef, quartered it, hung it up, and let customers cut off what they wanted with their own knives. Barney Beef is a recipe of the era, known commonly as a boiled dinner. Brisket later became the preferred cut for this all-in-one meal, cousin to New England's boiled dinner.

Pot roast should be lean, with some bone and a little fat. Trim excess fat to render for other use. Put meat into generous kettle and cover with boiling water. Cook at a slow perk until tender, 4 hours or more. A little shy of an hour before dinner time, add onions, carrots (and some add turnips or parsnips, but not James Barney), alternating over beef. About 20 minutes before serving time, quarter cabbage and core, then add to kettle. Season with salt and pepper. Cover and continue cooking but do not overcook. Vegetables should be tender, not mush. Put meat on big platter and arrange vegetables around it. Serve with mustard.

4 pounds pot roast
6 small onions, peeled
8 carrots, scraped
1 head cabbage, small
1 tablespoon salt
1 teaspoon pepper
boiling water with a pinch of salt

'Receipt To Care For Meat'

Charles and Lily Blaine arrived in Phoenix in November 1890 with their children, May and James. They had traveled by covered wagon from Cimmaron, Colorado, by way of Las Vegas, New Mexico, over the old Santa Fe Trail, according to Lily's old diary, *Fifty-six Days From Las Vegas to Phoenix.* Granddaughter Bobbie O'Haver saved their "meat receipt" but never used it.

To 1,000 pounds of meat take 14 quarts of salt, 3 pounds of brown sugar, 1 pound black pepper, 1 pound of saltpeter, dissolved in 1 quart of warm water, then mix all together. Make the salt wet enough to shape into balls. Rub the rind first, then flesh side. Lay wherever it will drain.
In 10 days it will be ready to hang up and smoke.

*Beef or venison was jerked to preserve it for later use, by Indians,
ranchers, and other early settlers. Apache Indians, in the Chiricahua
Mountains about 1900, have strung their venison between two
trees to dry.* SHARLOT HALL MUSEUM

Jerky

Jerky is the Indian's crude method of curing meat, similar to dried beef. Cut fresh meat in thin strips six to twelve inches in length, stripping off the tallow, and hang to dry either on horizontal poles, as the Indians did, or on wire. Usually the meat can be cured in several days without the aid of salt or smoke. When thoroughly dry, strips can be stored indefinitely.

Spanish Jerky, called "Carne Seca," is highly seasoned with vinegar, black pepper, and a little salt before drying. It is sometimes rubbed with garlic and sprinkled with red chili.

Pemmican is the jerked meat toasted over a fire until crisp, then pounded into a hash. Indians dug a hole in the ground, and a buffalo hide was staked over it to form a skin dish into which the meat was thrown to be pounded. Meanwhile, the marrow bones were split up and boiled in water until all the grease and oil came to the top, then skimmed off and poured over the pounded meat. As soon as cool, the mixture was sewed into skin bags and laid away until needed, sometimes buried or otherwise cached. Pemmican will keep indefinitely, is extremely nourishing, and agreeable to the taste.

From the United States Bureau of American Ethnology, 1892-93

Jerky Gravy, Tonto Basin Style

At age 89, Roxie Cline of Tonto Basin reflected that Jerky Gravy was the mainstay of the ranch at home and on roundups in the early days. Her husband, the late George Cline, built their ranch on the east side of Tonto Creek, which isolated it from "the world" when rains and melted snows made the creek rise so high even a horse couldn't swim it. The cook had to make do with what was on hand—dried meat.

"We always had jerky to keep us going, often three times a day," Roxie said. "Sometimes we jerked a deer and venison jerky is mighty tasty."

George Cline claimed that it made him sick to eat his own beef, in the then-classic mode of cattlemen, so he'd butcher a "stray" or "lost" animal. Besides, that kept him even with his similarly afflicted neighbors. Much of Roxie's life was spent cooking beef or game on roundups. Her "receipt" is prime for breakfast—when dawn is coloring the Sierra Ancha peaks; or lunch—when the cows are bushed up in the shade; or supper—when the Mazatzals darken.

Prepare jerky: Remove any dried rancid fat. Take hammer and pound jerky on hard rock until meat shreds.

Grease: Pour bacon grease or suet drippings into iron skillet on camp fire, amount depending on number of hungry cowpunchers you're feeding.

Flour: Throw into hot grease a half-handful of flour or more, depending on number of eaters. Stir flour and brown, brown, brown until it doggone near burns.

Milk: Mix canned milk with water, starting with a cup. Pour all at once into browned flour, stirring steadily to keep from lumping. Use enough milk to make smooth, shining gravy.

Seasoning: None. Jerked meat already has been salted and peppered generously when it was put out to dry.

Ready: Call the cowboys, with "Grub's on." Pour Jerky Gravy over hot Dutch oven biscuits.

As told to Marguerite Noble for use in Payson's *Centennial (1882-1982) Cookbook*, a historic little roundup of old photos and old recipes.

Red Flannel Hash

First came the corned beef, and as day follows night, then came the hash. When the Ladies Auxiliary of the Chloride Volunteer Fire Department shook out all the old recipes for the American Revolution Bicentennial, Jessie Handorth's hash made it into their cookbook as "plain rib-sticking good." Who first put beets in the hash is still in doubt.

Chop each ingredient separately, then mix together. Cook in well-greased skillet, heating slowly. As hash heats, loosen around the edges and shake back and forth to prevent scorching. When a nice brown crust forms on the bottom, turn out on a warmed plate and serve. If ingredients are dry enough to worry you, moisten with a little cream or beef broth. Old-timers greased the iron skillet they used with a little smoked bacon or salt pork, which added to the flavor. Serves 4.

1 ½ cups chopped corned beef
1 ½ cups chopped cooked beets
4 cups cooked chopped potatoes
1 medium onion, chopped

Coffee Roundup Roast

Lena Scholey Franks had a western-storybook childhood on a ranch on the Agua Fria below Mayer. Indian friends taught her how to build a pit fire, bake century plant and squaw bread. Once she discovered she had eaten baked wood rats and another time a horse that had been killed by the train. Her dad, George T. Scholey, was part of the family which established the first stage station at Camp Wood. Lena's most popular dish (not of Indian origin) was this tender, brown Coffee Roundup Roast.

Use a large knife to cut slits completely through 3 to 5 pounds of brisket. Insert slivers of garlic and onion. Pour 1 cup of vinegar over the meat. Work it down into the slits. Refrigerate, covered, to marinate 24 to 48 hours.

Lift into heavy iron or Dutch oven. Pour 2 cups strong black coffee over meat. Add 2 cups of water to cover. Simmer on top of stove 4 to 6 hours. Season to taste with salt and pepper 20 minutes before serving. If heat gets too high or lid is not tight enough, add water to retain moisture. Everyone who tasted this roast commented on the unusual and pleasing flavor.

3 to 5 pounds of brisket
slivers of garlic and onion
1 cup of vinegar
2 cups strong black coffee
2 cups of water to cover
salt and pepper to taste

Black Walnut Beef Roast

Mrs. Baron Goldwater, mother of Senator Barry Goldwater, was as inventive and as public-spirited as her son. Respected as a nurse, she was honored by Springerville; the town named its first hospital the Josephine Goldwater Hospital. The patients, however, never were put on a diet of her exceptional food, such as this walnut-studded, savory beef.

Trim fat from meat. Ground round is best ground twice. Make it into meat balls and refrigerate. Cover beef with broth in Dutch oven and top with onion halves. Cook slowly 4 hours or until tender. Skim off any fat. One hour before serving, add the meat balls and 1 jar of the pickled walnuts, which have been mashed with their juice. Just before serving, stir browned flour into pan juices and add the other 2 jars of walnuts. Taste and add salt and pepper, if needed. Serve with rice or noodles. Serves 8 memorably.

6 pounds chuck or any pot roast beef
1 pound ground round steak
1 large onion, halved
10 ounces beef broth
3 5-ounce jars pickled black walnuts
salt and pepper to taste
2 tablespoons browned flour

Hunt's Meat Curing Recipe

Although ranchers and farmers raised their own meat, there was still the problem of keeping it in edible condition over long periods. Mrs. L.B. Hunt of Taylor gave her method to the Northern Arizona Cowbelles for their Chuck Box Cook Book. *This is the best way meat was cured for winter by most pioneers.*

Boil together. Let cool. Add enough water to cover meat, which should be weighted down. Use either beef or pork, but a barrel for each kind. Double recipe for 200 pounds meat.

Mrs. Hunt cured fresh meat for jerky and fish with a salt crock at hand. For jerky, she dissolved all the salt possible in a kettle of boiling water, then dipped fresh meat strips into salt water a few seconds. Salt kept the flies away when jerky was hung over a stretched wire. Fish was preserved in layers of salt in a box. Both kept indefinitely if no moisture reached them.

For each 100 pounds meat, beef or pork, use:
6 pounds salt, No. 2
2 pounds brown sugar
3 ounces soda
2 ounces saltpeter
3 ounces black pepper

Sweetbreads From the Range to the Table

Sweetbread is not a bread; it's a meat. Its origin is not known to the average cook. Frances Mahan, historian of Kingman and the Pinta Ranch IKK, wrote this explanation in range language for the first *Chuck Box Cook Book:*

"Generally speaking, ranch folks do not go shopping for sweetbreads. Their hope lies in the animal they butcher—and let me warn you—sweetbread is not found in every critter out on the range—mainly in sucking calves—sometimes in yearlings, but not often. Then, too, if a calf's growth has been hampered by, say, the mother weathers a dry spell, she often gets hungry, sometimes failing in her milk. In other words, she's a poor suckler and dogies her calf. When the rains do come and grass gets good, she picks up, puts on weight and so does her calf. Sad to say, no matter how well Ma makes up, the calf's sweetbread production ended back there in the drouth, never to return.

"Ordinarily, butchering time is about sundown, assuming the beef is your own. Beef Killing Time attracts everything on the ranch, especially the dogs and cats. They gather around looking hungry and wistful. We'll omit the rest of the butchering except to find the sweetbread, which is on both sides of the jugular vein in the sticking place. Human anatomy calls it the pancreas.

"With the essential collected—wash well, place in a pan of cold water to stand overnight. This is good breakfast food. Next morning, remove membrane and allow one-half to one part per person. Cover with boiling water, allowing 1 teaspoon of salt and 1 tablespoon vinegar to 2 quarts water. Cover and simmer 15-20 minutes. Drain, cover with cold water. Cool to handle, then dip sweetbread in seasoned flour, then into the skillet, iron preferred. Brown in favorite shortening and eat at once, a real product of the range."

Western Ranch Meat Loaf

Ground meat was first mentioned in American cookbooks in 1902, as beef put twice through a meat grinder with onion and pepper. It became popular with rapidity and soon meat loaf was born, usually made of beef but where game was available, often a mixture of venison or elk and beef.

Lilliebelle Wilkerson hostessed cattlegrowers from around the state every August at the family ranch near Clifton. Her meat loaf was superb.

Make a stuffing of: 1 chopped onion and ¾ cup sliced celery browned in 2 tablespoons butter, then add ⅓ cup chopped green pepper, 1 teaspoon salt, 2 eggs, 3 cups dry bread crumbs, and enough water to mix. Add half of this stuffing to 2 pounds of ground beef. Mix well.

Put half the meat loaf mixture into a 2-quart loaf pan. Spread the stuffing over the meat. Top with remaining meat mixture. Bake in moderate oven about 350 degrees 1¼ hours.

Combine ½ cup tomato juice and 2 tablespoons melted butter. After loaf has baked 15 minutes, pour half this juice over the meat. Cook 15 minutes more, then pour remaining half of juice over the loaf. This adds flavor and keeps loaf moist. Serves 8.

1 chopped onion
¾ cup sliced celery
2 tablespoons butter
⅓ cup chopped green pepper
1 teaspoon salt
2 eggs
3 cups dry bread crumbs
water
2 pounds ground beef
½ cup tomato juice
2 tablespoons melted butter

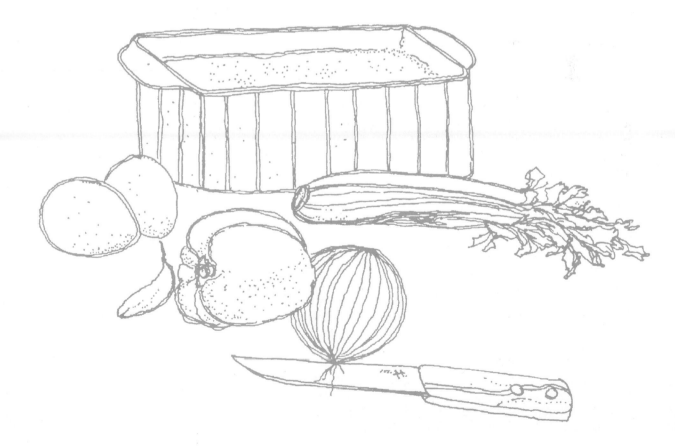

Cornish Pasties

The miners who came here from Wales, Scotland, and England took a pasty rather than a sandwich to lunch as solid nutritional reinforcement for cold, underground toil. This recipe is from an old Bisbee cookbook, but pasties were just as popular in the Globe-Miami regions.

Make up pastry from flour, salt, lard, and cold water, being careful not to make this too moist. Should hold together well enough to leave the sides of the bowl as mixed. Divide into four sections. Roll each out as for pie, ¼ inch thick. Keep as round as possible. Place on one half of a circle layer of thinly sliced potatoes and onions. Cover with beef, cut in medium pieces. Top with butter, salt, and pepper to taste. Fold unfilled half of crust over filling and seal by pinching with fingers or pressing tines of fork, to make a half-moon. Cut a small hole in the center of each. Bake about 30 minutes in a quick oven, 400 degrees or so.

Meat pies became popular with cowboys, too. Mrs. Margaret Smith of Holbrook, a Northern Arizona Cowbelle, called them Forfar Briddies.

When available, fresh parsley added flavor to pasties.

3 cups flour
½ teaspoon salt
1 cup lard
⅓ cup water, (approx.)
4 medium potatoes, pared
2 medium onions, sliced
1 pound beef round, no fat or gristle
butter, salt, and pepper

Sister's Country-Fried Steak

Eulalia (Sister) Bourne taught back-country schools for 50 years at Reddington, Helvetia, Manning's Ranch, Cierrita, Beaver Creek, and Baboquivari. She named every cow on her own small spread, the G-F Bar near Mammoth. When she took the exams for a teaching certificate, she borrowed $10, walked nine miles to Castle Hot Springs, took the stage to Congress Junction, rented a horse to ride into Phoenix, and spent two nights in a hotel—and she passed. The University of Arizona Press published three of her books about cows and kids, which interested her more than cooking. But the late Woman in Levis *(her most popular book) fried a great steak.*

Cut off fat and trim steak to serving-size pieces. Combine flour and salt and pepper in soup plate. Pound into meat with edge of saucer. Brown in bacon drippings in large iron pan or Dutch oven, adding onion as you turn meat. Pour tomatoes, canned or cooked, over meat and top with chile pepper. Cover and simmer 1 hour. Add water if necessary and cook another hour. For garlic eaters, a clove may be minced and added with onion. Many cooks call this Swiss Steak, but nobody has to be called twice for a helping.

2 pounds beef steak, venison, or elk
½ cup flour
salt and pepper to taste
¼ cup drippings
1 large onion, sliced
1 quart tomatoes
1 green chile pepper, optional
½ cup water

Bildots Costeletak Mocholonarekin Eta Biper Salsa

(Lamb Steaks with Mushrooms and Pimento Sauce)

This lamb recipe was widely circulated by Mrs. John Ale-man, the Spanish-Basque-speaking president of the Arizona Wool Growers Association in its heydey. The Basques emigrated here from Spain, France, and South America, settling primarily in the Flagstaff, Buckeye, and Casa Grande areas. About 200 families became citizens.

Broil lamb steaks 4 to 6 inches from the source of heat for 12 to 14 minutes, or until lightly browned on both sides. As lamb broils, prepare sauce in a skillet. Melt butter or warm the olive oil, then add mushrooms and cook no more than 5 minutes. Add flour, salt, and pepper and blend smooth. Gradually add milk. Cook over low heat, stirring constantly to sauce or gravy consistency, lightly bubbling. Add pimento and mix well. Drain well if using canned pimento. Serve piping hot over lamb chops.

5 lamb steaks, from the leg, about ¾ inch thick
4 tablespoons olive oil or butter
1 cup sliced mushrooms
4 tablespoons flour
¼ teaspoon pepper
1 teaspoon salt
2 cups milk
4 tablespoons diced pimento

Lamb or Mutton Stew

Mutton stew is a staple for both the Navajo and the Hopi sheep owners, but the Navajos have been confirmed herders to the greater extent because their reservation stretches infinitely farther. My stew lessons came from Inez Tewawina. She had a Navajo father and a Hopi mother and grew up "tending the sheeps so the wolfs could not get them." Spring lamb was usually cooked with spring greens, especially nanakopsie. Mutton was enhanced with hominy and dried red pepper. Sometimes Inez made a big pot of stew and put everything in. Delicious.

Remove fat from lamb and cut in bite-size pieces. Put in pot and cover with water. Bring to a boil and scoop off any scum. Add nanakopsie, crushed red pepper, and salt. Reduce heat, cover, and simmer 2 hours or more. Add hominy and cook over low heat all day, until kernels are skin-bursting tender. Serve in bowls with pieces of adobe bread for mopping the broth.

2 pounds young lamb, cut in chunks
water to cover
nanakopsie, if available, a handful
6 to 8 cups hominy
1 dried red chile pepper, crushed fine
salt

Maddock Baked Ham

Jean Wallace Maddock was one of the organizers of the First Families of Arizona, pioneers who settled here before statehood, and suggested the name for the group. She liked to "cook something different," originating this simple way of enhancing ham.

Use a center slice of ham, 1½ to 2 inches thick. Spread mustard lightly on the top surface, sprinkle with pepper, brown sugar, and flour. Pour milk in the pan up the the edge of the ham, so that as it boils, it spreads over the top of the ham slice, making a delicious crust.

Stuffed Pork Chops

Pork chops, cut 1½ inches to 2 inches thick, were often slit to form a pocket which was filled with the family's favorite bread stuffing. On the T Bar Ranch in Snowflake, Mrs. Vern L. Willis stuffed them with sweet potatoes—a meal in one chop.

Chops must be thick. Cut pockets lengthwise through center to bone for the stuffing. Season to taste with salt and pepper. Stuff with mixture of sweet potatoes, apples, salt and pepper to taste, and the egg. Fasten the edges around with toothpicks. Dip chops in milk and roll in bread crumbs. Bake in greased pan for 1½ hours or until tender at 350 degrees.

6 large trimmed pork chops
milk and bread crumbs
2 cups mashed sweet potatoes
1 cup raw apples, chopped
salt and pepper to taste
1 egg, beaten

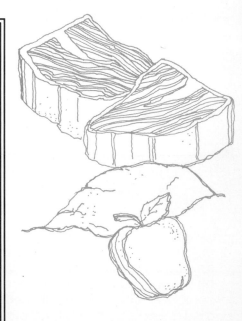

Pork and the Law

In 1877, the Arizona Territorial Legislature passed a law prohibiting hogs from running loose in any town. Some rugged individuals, such as Pete Kitchen of the Nogales-Tubac area, penned up their pigs to keep the Apaches from making pincushions of them. Pete's hams were the most desired in the territory. In many small towns, pigs ran loose, leaving a wake of dirt and destruction, although they were kept to eat garbage rather than make it. One devious old Ehrenberg character, Justice of the Peace Tom Hamilton, solved his pig-keeping problems by loading them onto his ferry and locating them in California on what is now the Blythe flats.

Sausage

On the many farms and ranches where pigs were part of the stock, the coming of fall meant butchering. Fresh sausage was the most popular by-product, although scrapple and head cheese (made from the hog's head) were appreciated by those who could put them together. Pickled pig's feet were prized, too—but not by everyone.

Sprinkle spices and salt over meat which has been cut in strips. Put meat through grinder or the finest blade of the food chopper. Mix well. Put into pans or other vessels that can be covered. Store in cold place. Cut off as desired to make sausage cakes. A person could do a hard morning's work after a breakfast of this sausage and pancakes, as made and served at the Sundown Ranch in Aripine.

12 pounds lean pork (part beef or game may be used)
6 pounds fat pork
8 tablespoons sage
2 tablespoons black pepper
4 teaspoons cloves
2 teaspoons nutmeg
4 tablespoons salt

Roast Venison

Use a tender cut from the leg, loin, or rib. Lard (wrap slices of larding pork around the meat, or pierce meat and push strips into incisions) and sprinkle with salt, pepper, and flour. Roast at 350 degrees until medium-rare, which gives the best flavor and most tender meat. Baste often with melted bacon fat. Last half-hour, place scrubbed and peeled potatoes, carrots, and onions around meat. For added flavor, crush three or four juniper berries and add to pot. Because venison is such a lean meat, it should be cooked slowly, with fat and possibly ¼ cup of hot water—best from teakettle. Do not add cold water.

Venison and Noodles

In a skillet, gently sauté the onion in 3 tablespoons of butter until tender. Add 3 more tablespoons of butter and sauté the mushrooms for 3 to 5 minutes. Add seasoning to taste, then remove from pan and keep warm. Add remaining butter to pan and brown the floured meat strips. Add broth and simmer no more than 5 minutes. Add the onion-mushroom mixture and the sour cream, if desired. Heat gently. Serve over hot, buttered noodles. Sprinkle with paprika or parsley, if a dash of color is needed.

1 large onion, finely chopped
7 tablespoons butter
4 or 5 large, fresh mushrooms
salt and pepper to taste
1½ pounds venison, cut into 3 ½-inch strips, floured
1 cup beef stock
1 cup sour cream, optional
3 cups hot, buttered noodles

Jugged Venison, Elk, or Bear

The confirmed game eater knows that the way the meat is treated immediately after the kill is the first secret of good flavor. The second secret is lucking out on the age of the game: the younger, the better. With an older animal, William B. Farrow of Cottonwood, an expert in game cookery, jugged the meat.

Take 1 quart dry wine (red or white), preferably sherry. Into that, put a whole onion, 3 buttons garlic, pinch of dill seed, 12 whole peppercorns, 6 bay leaves, and ½ cup vinegar.

Immerse shoulder of venison, elk, or bear—or any less tender cut—for 3 days in this wine mixture.

Drain and place meat in a roaster pan. Put in enough marinade, strained, to make about 1 inch of liquid in the pan. Simmer very slowly until meat begins to fall off the bones.

Soak steaks in the same marinade for 2 or 3 hours before pan broiling in butter. Do not use too much butter or grease. Remove the steak when browned but juicy, to hot platter. Pour a little marinade into the pan and stir to take up bits of steak and make a sauce or, as Farrow said, a *sauce chasseur*.

Courtesy of Arizona Cowbelles.

1 quart dry wine (red or white), preferably sherry
1 whole onion
3 buttons garlic
pinch of dill seed
12 whole peppercorns
6 bay leaves
½ cup vinegar
butter

(LEFT) Sharlot Hall, Arizona's premier poetess-historian, was equally adept with powder and pen. She bagged this deer in December 1906.
SHARLOT HALL MUSEUM

French Fried Diamondback

There were Penrods throughout the Show Low-Lakeside area with roots stretching back to the late 1800s, all Mormon and all good cooks. The wildest recipe from any of them was Joy Penrod's for diamondback rattlesnake.

The best time to catch a rattlesnake is in early spring, just before they leave their dens of hibernation. With the utmost care and caution, catch a rattler, using a snare. Don't settle for one less than two feet in length.

Continuing to use snare and long-handled pole, kill the snake by chopping off the head. It is best to have help standing by. Hang by rattlers on a pole.

Using a sharp knife, slit the stomach side. Remove layer of fat just under skin and eviscerate carcass. Wash in deep pan of cool water. Be certain pan is large because the water changes the temperature of the muscles, causing the carcass to contract and move around, sometimes vigorously, for a few minutes.

Cut meat into 3-inch pieces. Roll each piece in a mixture of salt, pepper, flour, and fine cracker crumbs. Drop into wire basket and submerge in boiling hot cooking oil, in deep fryer or deep iron skillet. Cook no more than 5 minutes until golden brown.

Serve with pickles, hot peppers, and potato chips for an unforgettable meal. Serves 2 or 3, depending on the size of the snake and the open-minded attitude of those eating.

3-inch slices of rattlesnake
flour and cracker crumbs
salt and pepper
hot cooking oil

Roast Haunch of Javelina

L. D. Clark, novelist and professor of English at the University of Arizona for many years, was an authority on English novelist and poet D. H. Lawrence, and a specialist in game cookery. Nobody refused to eat his javelina.

In a turkey roaster, brown the haunch in half-cup of rendered salt pork or desired shortening. Pepper meat on both sides. Add onions, garlic, and mushrooms. Sprinkle with fines herbes. Cover the meat with slices of salt pork from which most of the salt has been soaked out in hot water. Cover roaster and roast at 300 degrees for 4 or 5 hours. No British king had better.

As with all game, wild hog or javelina must be cleaned and skinned at once and the meat chilled through. It can be served as barbecued ribs, breaded cutlets, ham steaks, roasted, or baked.

1 haunch of javelina
pepper to taste
3 purple onions, sliced
3 to 5 buttons of garlic, sliced
½ pound fresh mushrooms
fines herbes
1 cup hot water
6 to 8 slices salt pork, soaked

Greenlee County Pan-Broiled Bear Steak

There is no reason why hunters should waste any part of the bear, as all of the meat is edible, and these recipes should be of help.

Pan-broiled steak is a very delicious dish. Trim fat from steak, also part of bone, if desired. Wipe with damp cloth. Heat frying pan until very hot. Rub surface of pan with a little fat. Place steak in pan, sear quickly, first one side and then the other, turning every 10 seconds. After both sides are browned, reduce heat and cook slowly. If desired well done, it will require from 15 to 20 minutes longer.

If you should be in camp, take a Dutch oven and cut a chuck roast from the bear. Let simmer for several hours and it will be just as tender as any piece of beef steer meat. Or, you can make a bear stew with various cuts of rump.

At home, you can grind the meat, making meat balls, and serve with cream sauce or any sauce which suits your taste—wine, horseradish, or hot.

Edited from *William (Bill) Petersen's Cookbook*, long out of print.

Squirrel Stew

Nobody in Arizona has more authentic memories of the author Zane Grey than the Babe Haught family of the Tonto Rim area. From 1918 to 1929, Grey brought his son and his Japanese cook to be guided by Anderson Lee (Babe) Haught. At first, they lived in the hand-hewn, two-story Haught homestead, now listed for historic preservation. Then Grey had his own home built on a site to capture the Mogollon Rim view he grew to love, writing, "For wild, rugged beauty, I had not seen its equal." With hot camp biscuits, one of his favorite meals was squirrel stew. Squirrel meat is light-colored, fine-textured, with mild flavor.

3 squirrels, cleaned and cut into serving pieces
½ cup butter
2 onions, sliced
2 tablespoons wine or cider vinegar
1 pinch thyme
salt and pepper to taste
2 tablespoons flour
1 cup cold water

Melt butter in big cast iron Dutch oven. Brown squirrel pieces on all sides. Do not cook, just brown. Remove and brown onions, then add vinegar and seasonings, stirring well. Return squirrel pieces to Dutch oven and add enough water to almost cover meat. Cover and cook 1 hour, then reduce heat. In today's kitchen oven, begin at 350 degrees and cut to 315. Mix flour in cold water until there are no lumps, after squirrel has baked about 2 hours. Stir into pot, and keep stirring about 10 minutes until it bubbles into a thin gravy. Serve squirrel over hot biscuits with lots of gravy. Yes, there are bones. Eat slowly and remove bones as you go.

Chapter 7
Fish and Feathers

The mountains and the deserts of Arizona made up a happy hunting ground for turkey, dove, wild duck, geese, quail, and pigeon—cooked over the fire, mud-daubed and in the coals, or simmered in the pot. Later, wine and bread crumbs added allure.

Although today there are more than sixty species of fish in our waters, less than half are native. There is only one native game fish, the yellow-gold Arizona trout. Trout-addicted diners maintain it is best fresh-caught and butter-browned, crisp enough to eat the tail.

It is difficult to believe, but some of the most dedicated fisherman in the world live on the desert, just dreaming of weekends fishing for bass, channel cat, perch, crappie, and bluegills. Dams, floods, droughts, and population growth kept altering the fishing picture.

Another almost unbelievable bit of seafood history involves the oyster, always the hit of the boom towns. Old ads lauded oysters fresh from Baltimore, washed down with champagne—possible in Prescott, Jerome, Bisbee, or Tombstone. Ice and sawdust did the trick.

As for chicken and turkey, Grandma always had chickens, whether she lived in town or out, which meant eggs for breakfast and fried chicken the like of which today's children may never taste. Chicken biscuit pie, chicken pot pie, or noodles and chicken broth were pioneer pleasure, as well as good medicine. Turkey, then as now, made Thanksgiving a day to be reckoned with.

John Slaughter was only five feet four inches tall. But as a former Texas Ranger turned Arizona sheriff, he brought peace to Cochise County in three short years—1887 to 1890. Cattle rustlers and train robbers vamoosed, and the Apaches learned to avoid his territory. Yet it was the prospect of ranching in Southeastern Arizona and Northern Sonora, Mexico, that brought John and Viola Slaughter to the San Bernardino Valley in the 1880s.

The ranch they first leased, then bought, sprawled over approximately 70,000 acres, about two-thirds of it in Mexico. A land grant dating back many years, El Rancho de San Bernardino, had been deserted nearly fifty years because of troublesome Apaches who made ranching a hazardous and unprofitable pursuit.

His 30,000 cattle carried the first registered brand in Cochise County. Artesian wells irrigated five hundred acres of grains and vegetables. He built a generous home with wide, cool verandas, replacing one destroyed by an earthquake. Another adobe house was built for his wife's parents.

Ideal for the secluded life, the San Bernardino

Ranch nevertheless had many noteworthy visitors through the years. The infamous Geronimo had been on the ranch, as had Pancho Villa. So had such distinguished guests as General John J. Pershing and Senator Henry Fountain Ashurst.

Although it was a working ranch, the main dining room was distinguished by fine linen, silver, and china services. Visiting cowboys who were grimy from a day's work usually chose to eat in the separate cowboy dining room.

Baking at the ranch, Historian Reba B. Wells wrote, meant thirty-four loaves of bread daily. Meat and milk were produced on the ranch, but tubs of butter came from Douglas, the nearby town that Slaughter had helped develop. Canning, preserving, winemaking, and brandying were regular occupations. No visitor to the San Bernardino Ranch could escape being warmly welcomed and bountifully fed.

The San Bernardino Ranch, a National Historic Landmark, is operated by the Johnson Historic Museum of the Southwest, and open to the public.

Dutch Oven Wild Turkey

Colonel William Greene of Cananea, Mexico, and Arizona was a born showman, a mining developer, and always in need of money. He brought financiers from Wall Street into the wilds of the Sierra Madres and had their meals cooked in Dutch ovens. As they rode from camp to camp, they killed bear, venison, and turkey, then drank champagne or tequila while the camp cooks tamed the wild meat.

A decent-sized bird took three or four hours to cook, so Colonel Bill had masseurs and barbers at hand from one of New York's best places.

After turkey has been dressed and drawn, stuff with corn bread dressing, made by mixing ingredients at right.

Truss turkey and lay on back in Dutch oven. Dredge with flour, salt, and pepper, and dot with butter. As soon as flour is browned, reduce heat, cover, and roast. Keep a willing eye on turkey, adding hot water only, not cold, if needed to keep turkey from getting dry.

1 onion, chopped
1 cup celery, chopped
¼ cup butter or bacon drippings
6 cups crumbled corn bread
1 teaspoon sage
salt and pepper to taste
2 eggs
½ cup water, whiskey, or rum

Turkey en Casserole

The Arizona homemaker's love affair with the casserole dish grew steadily through the '20s and '30s. Combinations like this were especially popular for after-the-holidays turkey.

Sauté mushrooms in butter; drain and add flour to butter. Blend until smooth; add broth, celery, mushrooms, chestnuts, sherry, and salt. Mix with turkey. Arrange in buttered casserole. Place in pan of water and bake at 400 degrees 25-30 minutes or until bubbling. Especially tasty with a topping of toasted almonds, sliced.

A similar recipe was served over patty shells at many resort hotels and was a favorite of Isabella Selmes Greenway, a pioneer in the winter visitor business. She had built the Arizona Inn in Tucson and was the only woman to represent Arizona in the United States Congress (1933-36).

¼ cup sliced mushrooms
4 tablespoons butter
1 tablespoon flour
1¼ cups turkey broth
½ cup chopped, cooked celery
4 sliced water chestnuts
3 tablespoons sherry wine
salt to taste
1 pinch nutmeg, optional
2 to 3 cups cooked, diced turkey

Helen's Hot Chicken Salad

In the early 1900s, John Jay Fagan married Helen Hirst when he was a cashier at the Central Bank (long gone) in Phoenix. He acquired almost for a song a small mountain of Sunnyslope land which the family, grown to George, Robert, John, and Harriet, helped homestead. They carried water by bucket to put out crops. Helen ran an idea kitchen for Fannin Gas (also gone) and had a radio recipe show. One of her most popular ideas was crunchy chicken salad, hot OR cold. Helen preferred the flavor of roasted chicken for salad.

Sliver almonds or cashews and mix with cut-up chicken (or turkey) and celery, salt, onion, and mayonnaise. Pile into casserole or sea shells. Sprinkle chips with cheese on top. Bake 15 minutes at 450 degrees until thoroughly hot, yet retaining celery crispness. Mix in grapes. Delicious with cranberry-orange molded salad.

2 cups cooked chicken, cut up
2 cups celery, cut fine
½ cup toasted almonds or cashews
½ teaspoon salt
2 tablespoons grated onion
1 cup mayonnaise
1 cup crushed potato chips
½ to ¾ cup sharp cheese, grated
seedless grapes

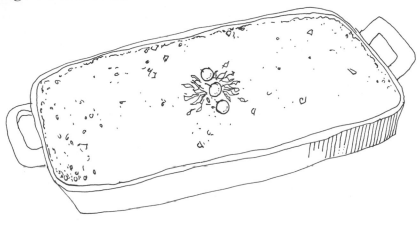

Lucy's Pressed Chicken

Lucy Kelly lived in Bisbee when the Depression caused the mines to go on a three-day work week. "My husband, Edward Carl, was a boss. He earned forty-five dollars every two weeks. Nobody paid any attention to the stock market except Phelps Dodge. Life was good. No one had any money so we all made do. I'd take a look at my chickens and, when it was hot, the oldest wound up pressed."

Boil an old rooster, or a hen which isn't laying eggs, at a slow roll until meat comes off the bones. Pour off the liquid and boil it down some. Skim fat off the broth when cold. Pick meat off bones into small bits. Press down into a deep dish. Cover with the chicken broth and let set overnight. Slice and serve with mashed potatoes, green salad, and a vegetable. For fancy occasions, pipe a ruffle of mayonnaise around the top of the chicken, unmolded on a platter.

Chicken and Noodles

A plump hen and her eggs and a cup of flour made a hearty, comforting meal for generations, as told in crisp directions by Capitola Dickey for the Pine-Strawberry roundup of treasured recipes.

Cut up chicken. Dice carrot, onion, and celery. Place in pot with bay leaf, salt, and pepper to taste in water to cover. Bring to a boil, then simmer until chicken is tender. Cool and take chicken off bone, if you prefer. While chicken cooks, make egg noodles and roll thin to dry. When dry, cut and drop into boiling chicken. Simmer until tender, 10 to 15 minutes.

Egg Noodles: Combine egg and salt. Add enough flour to make a stiff dough. Roll out very thin on floured board or pastry cloth. Let stand 20 or 30 minutes until partially dry. (My mother-in-law, Blanche DeWald, rolled out miles of noodle dough over the years, hanging it across our long dining room table, and every time she said, "I can never roll dough as thin as my mother did.") Either roll up and slice in ⅛-inch strip or cut in squares. Drop a few at a time into boiling chicken broth.

1 frying-size chicken
1 medium onion
2 stalks celery
1 large carrot
1 bay leaf
salt and pepper
Egg Noodles:
2 eggs, beaten
½ teaspoon salt
1 cup flour, more if needed

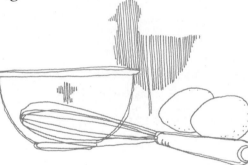

Oven Omelet

Bessie Thompson Lipinski grew up in the zig-zag of Jerome and the Verde Valley. She was of English ancestry, the line of Mary, Queen of Scots. After a career teaching English and a happy marriage to Aaron, she discovered a fresh way to use old family recipes by bringing Bed and Breakfast to Arizona. Oven Omelet did not come, originally, with diced green chiles. They just seem to sneak into Arizona recipes.

Fry bacon in iron skillet until just crisp. Remove and drain well. Reserve only 1 tablespoon of drippings. Add onion and cook until clear on low heat. Keep warm. Beat eggs, cream, salt, and mace with fork, just enough to blend. Fold in parsley, cheese, and chiles (if guests are game). Pour mixture into warm skillet over bacon. Bake 15 minutes in oven preheated to 350 degrees. Cut into 6 pie wedges and serve with warm tortillas.

6 slices lean bacon, 1-inch cuts
¼ cup minced onion and tops
7 eggs
½ cup cream
salt to taste
pinch of mace
2 tablespoons minced parsley
1 cup grated sharp cheese
½ cup diced green chiles

Almond Chicken

There were Chinese in Phoenix and Glendale from the area's earliest days. Although there was some discrimination, they operated all of the restaurants in 1911 except one. They also controlled many of the truck gardens. Those Chinese pioneers persevered to become professional and mercantile leaders.

Mix first five ingredients. Marinate diced chicken in mixture, then sprinkle with cornstarch. Mix well and set aside. Heat oil in large pan, adding vegetables a few at a time. Cook about 5 minutes, stirring lightly. Fry chicken mixture in hot pan, stirring constantly until white and cooked. Add vegetables and onions and cook a minute or two. Sprinkle with almonds and serve hot at once.

2 tablespoons soy sauce
1 tablespoon whiskey
1 tablespoon sugar
1 teaspoon salt
1 teaspoon chopped ginger root
1 to 2 pounds chicken, diced
2 tablespoons cornstarch
3 tablespoons sesame oil
1 4-ounce can bamboo shoots, diced
½ cup water chestnuts, diced
1 cup celery hearts, diced
½ pound fresh snow peas
1 4-ounce can mushrooms
2 green onions, diced
½ cup roasted almonds

Egg Butter

Sorghum was an important forage crop for sheep and cattle during the settling of the Southwest. Sweet sorghum, sometimes called sorgos, was made into molasses and became popular until sugar was made available at a reasonable price. Mayme Spurlock of Globe knew how to mix eggs with sorghum for dressing up hot biscuits or pancakes.

Cook 1 cup sorghum with 1 cup of sugar till it's thick. Stir in 2 eggs, well beaten, and a half-teaspoon of nutmeg. Cook for 15 minutes over slow fire, stirring once or twice. Very good with hot biscuits.

1 cup sorghum
1 cup sugar
2 eggs
½ teaspoon nutmeg

Red Pickled Eggs

Pickled eggs were part of the free lunch in saloon days, but eggs which made the picnic scene were a different matter. These came in fruit jars or gallons of ruby red beets in a pickle brine which transformed hard-boiled eggs into tender jewels. Pickled too long, they turn rubbery. I got this recipe in Brewery Gulch, Bisbee, from a German couple named Wertz, who insisted this pickle juice could be used twice, or more.

Drain the beets and reserve the juice. Quarter the beets and place them in a gallon jar. Boil the vinegar and the beet juice, then add remaining ingredients except for the eggs. Heat and stir to boiling point, then pour over beets. With wooden spoon, add eggs, one at a time, spacing throughout jar. When jars cool, cover and refrigerate. Serve eggs with little forks. Use eggs grated over beets in herring salad. Never try to sneak a pickled egg from the jar. That telltale red color is hard to wash away.

2 quarts canned beets
1 cup sharp vinegar
1 cup beet juice
½ cup sugar
3 cloves
salt and peppercorns
1 sliced onion
1 sliced red or green pepper
1 teaspoon horseradish
1 bay leaf
1 cinnamon stick
1 dozen hard-boiled eggs, shelled

Pinal County White Wing Dinner

William (Bill) Petersen spent the 1930s searching the state for recipes from the wild side of life—fish and game, that is. He was taught the culinary arts in a family of chefs, but World War I injuries kept him from following the profession. Still, he collected and published several volumes of a Cactus Barrel Full of Arizona Recipes, *which became little collector's items. They also got him a seat at some extraordinary dinners, like this one cooked by Mrs. Ruth J. Branaman, Pinal County treasurer.*

White Wings and Giblet Gravy
Baked Potatoes   Lettuce-Tomato Salad   Asparagus Tips
Hot Biscuits   Honey   Jersey Cow Butter
Arizona Iced Watermelon

Dress 12 white wings. Save livers, hearts, and gizzards. Rub birds with a mixture of salt, pepper, and paprika, 1 teaspoon of each, blended in olive oil. Place in hot skillet. Fry until tender, then remove birds to a warm platter. Add a little more oil, then place liver, hearts, and gizzards, chopped fine, in the skillet and sauté until tender. Makes a fine country gravy to cover the birds and to serve on the side.

1 dozen white wing doves
1 teaspoon each of salt, pepper, and paprika
olive oil

Hunting was never strictly a man's pursuit, particularly when it meant food for the table. SHARLOT HALL MUSEUM

Stuffed Squab

Betty Louise Kruse was born in 1926 in Deaconess (now Good Samaritan) Hospital in Phoenix. She and her twin, Rudy, were the tenth and eleventh children of Fred and Dorothy Kruse, who owned a farm and dairy. Betty picked and tied vegetables, separated milk, went to market, and loved to go hunting with her brothers, where she was valued for her cooking. This recipe can be adjusted for game birds or spring chicken.

Clean squab and chop giblets (heart, gizzard, liver, and neck, as desired). Some cooks like to simmer giblets in seasoned water until tender. Rub squab inside and out with a little salt and pepper. Fold wings back and brown in hot butter with onion. Remove squab; brown crumbs and chopped giblets, then add milk and seasonings. Stuff birds with this mixture and rub outside with melted butter or a little bacon fat. With game birds, a piece of bacon may be placed over each. Sprinkle lightly with flour and place birds in roasting pan. Cover and roast 45 minutes to an hour at 325 degrees, basting often with drippings and melted butter. Remove cover last 20 minutes. Birds will fall off the bone. Serve with potatoes or rice and biscuits to capture every bit of gravy.

6 squab
squab giblets, chopped
3 tablespoons butter
½ cup hot milk
1 tablespoon chopped onion
1 teaspoon salt
3 cups chopped bread crumbs
¼ teaspoon each, sage and pepper
flour and bacon fat

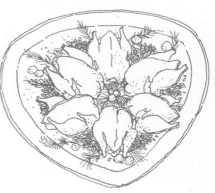

Lake Mead Baked Bass

Mrs. A. M. Cook, wife of the Mohave County treasurer during the '30s, when Lake Mead was filling 115 miles behind just-built Boulder (now Hoover) Dam, made a superb dish of lake bass, then further graced it with a port wine sauce.

Clean and dry bass. Spread chopped onion and half the cheese over bottom of large skillet which will accommodate fish. Place bass over cheese and onion. Add mustard, sauce, salt, and pepper to milk. Stir, then pour over fish. Sprinkle with freshly chopped parsley. Bake at 400 degrees 25 to 30 minutes. Serve with parsley potatoes, a cucumber salad, and this garnet-clear sauce.

Port Wine Sauce: Simmer 4 cloves and 1 cup fish or beef stock for 20 minutes. Combine ½ glass currant jelly, ½ glass port wine, ½ teaspoon salt, 2 tablespoons lemon juice, and a speck of cayenne pepper. Strain stock over mixture, removing cloves. Remove fish from from pan and combine wine sauce with the gravy.

2½ pounds Lake Mead bass
1 large onion, chopped fine
1 cup cheddar cheese, shredded
1 cup milk
1 teaspoon mustard
1½ teaspoons Worcestershire sauce
salt and pepper to taste
chopped parsley

Colorado River Catfish

William (Bill) Petersen recovered from World War I injuries while fishing and hunting along the Colorado River, during the 1930s. He made many friends sharing recipes. In one of the resulting original Arizona cookbooks, he dealt with that unlikely delicacy, the catfish.

There are approximately thirty-five different kinds of catfish. Some are called blue catfish, yellow cat, mud cat, flannel mouth, bull head, and various other names, but the best of this tribe is the channel catfish found in the riffles of the Colorado River.

Once caught, the preparation is very simple. Skin, draw, and wash and it is ready for the skillet. The backbone is the only bone to worry about! A choice way to prepare the catfish is to dip into a milk-and-egg batter, cover with cornmeal, and fry until done. Served with a well-seasoned tomato sauce (salsa) or Arizona lemon butter sauce. The channel cat may also be boiled and used for many other fish dishes. The choice catfish is 15 inches in length.

The mud cat, also found in our state, is of a stronger taste. After skinning and cleaning a mud fish, allow to stand in cold water with a little vinegar an hour or two. The mud cat is delectable baked. Prepare a mixture of paprika, cayenne, salt, pepper, and vinegar. Rub well into fish. Bake in hot oven and serve with any fish sauce desired.

Channel Catfish

skinned catfish
milk-and-egg cornmeal batter
tomato sauce (salsa) or Arizona lemon butter sauce

Mud Catfish

skinned catfish
cold water with a little vinegar
paprika, cayenne, salt pepper, and vinegar

Robert's Baked Fish

Robert Veazey, son of Eunice Babbitt Veazey of Northern Arizona's Babbitt family, inherited a strong interest in history. He collected Indian baskets and old Army memorabilia. Wife Sally began collecting, too, of necessity—fish recipes, when she discovered he ate, slept, talked and breathed fishing. This recipe can also be used for wild fowl. "Then call it the General's Duck," Bob said.

Arrange onions on large baking dish. Place fish on onions. Add remaining ingredients. Cover and bake 2 hours or until flake-tender but not overdone in 350-degree oven. Recipe is superb using any large fish.

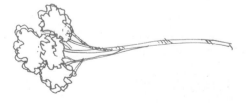

1 large bass, 3 to 5 pounds, cleaned
2 thinly sliced onions
6 whole peppercorns
2 bay leaves
2 quartered cloves of garlic
2 sprigs fresh parsley
1 cup dry vermouth
1 tablespoon ginger, grated fresh
salt, thyme, and rosemary to taste

Castle Hot Springs Fish Sauce

In 1865, Colonel Charles Craig, commander of troops at Prescott's Fort Whipple, defeated a band of marauding Apaches near the source of their "magic waters." Hot mineral waters tumbled from castles of rock in the Bradshaws, flowing at the rate of what later was proven to be 400,000 gallons a day. Named Castle Hot Springs, the spot became the dowager of Arizona resorts, visited by Teddy Roosevelt, the Vanderbilts, the Astors, the Fords, and other eminent families. They came by private railroad car to Phoenix, then by a five-hour stagecoach journey with three changes of horses. There were no kitchens in the cottages. The hotel staff, which equaled the guests in numbers, served meals in a many-windowed dining room. Such a remarkable place had to serve remarkable food. This fish sauce is an example.

1 pint vinegar
3 pints red port
plenty of shallots
horseradish
2 tablespoons pepper
½ lemon
2 or 3 anchovies
2 or 3 bay leaves
butter

Take rather more than a pint of vinegar, 3 pints of red port, plenty of shallots and horseradish, and 2 tablespoons of pepper, pounded very fine. Add the peel of half a lemon, 2 or 3 anchovies, and the same number of bay leaves. Let the whole boil together until the anchovies are dissolved, then strain. When cold, put into bottles. Two or 3 spoonfuls are sufficient per pound of butter for an elegant fish sauce.

Fire destroyed the Victorian elegance of the three-storied yellow-and-white hotel and with it most of the cookbooks and recipes. A few were printed in *The Arizona Republican*, an early Phoenix newspaper, including this fish enhancer.

The "catch of the day" by a Yavapai County rancher's wife, fishing in Granite Creek about 1900, would become the main course of that evening's dinner.
SHARLOT HALL MUSEUM

Hangtown Fry

From African Violet and Caliche to Sun and Soil and Valle del Sol, women's garden groups grew as fast as the Phoenix area expanded. They eventually cooperated to build a Valley Garden Center, raising funds with, of course, a cookbook, crammed with family favorites. Mrs. Walter Oliver traced the history of this recipe back to Gold Rush Days.

Drain 12 large oysters; roll in fine, dry bread crumbs. Season with salt and pepper. Dip in slightly beaten egg, then into crumbs again.

Melt ½ cup of butter in skillet. Add oysters and cook over medium heat until temptingly brown on both sides.

Beat 6 eggs, adding ½ teaspoon salt and ¼ cup milk. Pour over oysters and cook over low heat, lifting from bottom of pan and sides as it cooks. Avoid constant stirring, though. Cook until eggs are set but still moist.

Turn out on a large, warm serving plate and garnish with crisp bacon strips. Serve with sourdough toast.

1 dozen large oysters
bread crumbs
salt and pepper
slightly beaten egg
½ cup butter
6 eggs, beaten
½ teaspoon salt
¼ cup milk
garnish

Gefilte Fish

Until the 1950s, except for several fish markets, the best time to get store-bought fish was on Thursday—shipped in because Friday was a no-meat day for Catholics. Furthermore, Gefilte Fish, frequently served in Jewish homes on Friday night, was traditionally made with freshwater fish. Rose Levy of Phoenix, known for exceptional food, made Gefilte this way.

Chop fish fillets together. Add eggs, matzo meal, 1 chopped onion, salt, pepper, and water. Blend well, mix into balls, drop into boiling water to which carrots, celery, and other onion have been added. Cook very slowly 2 hours. Add 1 teaspoon sugar to broth, if desired. Serve garnished with the carrots and celery and horseradish.

3 pounds pike
1 mullet
1 small whitefish
2 eggs
½ cup matzo meal or bread crumbs
2 medium onions
2 carrots
2 pieces celery
salt and pepper to taste
½ cup water

Chapter 8
Served on the Side

*F*oods grown along the rivers and in the rich, rewarding native soil, high land or low, have fed Arizona's dwellers in amounts ranging from barely enough to overwhelming.

The not-so-secret ingredient has always been water; from rain, snow, or irrigation. Indians danced and prayed for it. Pioneers dug by hand, cussed, or prayed for it. Today, the farmer and rancher battle the land developer for it. The state's agricultural scene keeps shifting.

We began with beans, squash, and corn, then hay and pumpkins. After the Reclamation Act of 1902 and the birth of six dams, we farmed in all corners. The Arizona State Fair in 1953 received more than 2,000 entries in the Agriculture and Horticulture Departments: peaches from Oak Creek, apples from Verde Valley and Willcox, onions from Safford, peppers from San Simon, corn from Navajo County, pumpkins and squash from Springerville, dates, nuts, and citrus from Maricopa County, watermelon from Graham and Gila Counties, pears from Gila, and cotton, grains, and alfalfa from almost all of the state's then-14 counties. Bountiful iceberg lettuce greened in three or four separate seasons.

Backyard gardens were a part of our heritage. For Mormons, as for Father Kino, gardens, orchards, and grains were part of the fortification. Historian James H. McClintock wrote, quoting F. S. Dellenbaugh: "As pioneers the Mormons were superior to any class . . . their idea being homemaking and not skimming the cream off the country with a six-shooter and a whiskey bottle. One of the first things the Mormon always did was to plant fruit, shade trees, and vines, so that in a very few years there was a condition of comfort. They set a plentiful table."

Their counterparts among the Indians were the Hopis, who produced remarkable harvests from an arid land and still grow their corn, peaches, and chile peppers.

Acknowledging constant seesawing in the production of foods grown, Arizona's cooks accumulated the best possible recipes for using and preserving our vegetables, fruits, nuts, and grains. This collection mirrors the distant past and the hardscrabble times, reflecting vitality and richness in home cooking of Arizona produce from apples to zucchini.

---

*T*he impressive Flagstaff residence built for the Michael and Timothy Riordan families in 1904 apparently is the largest private residence ever built in Northern Arizona.

The unusual duplex mansion has undergone virtually no modification since it was built. It came directly from the Riordan family to the State of Arizona, without intervening ownership, was nominated to the National Register of Historic Sites in 1979, and became a State Historic Park the following year.

Michael, in particular, contributed ideas to the design of the home they called Kinlichi Knoll. Many of them—such as the massive stone arches at the porch corners, wings angled from each other, and rustic exterior combining logs, planks, stones, and shingles—

can also be seen at Grand Canyon's famous El Tovar Hotel. Architect Charles Whittlesey designed both buildings, and Michael Riordan came up with the name El Tovar. Kinlichi is a Navajo word for "red house," and the house drew its name from its original color, a dull, brick-red stain. The building contains thirty-five rooms, with 13,000 square feet of living space. Noteworthy during its era, the house has eight bathrooms. Also, it was built with a complete electrical system, unusual for its day.

Each side has its own well-equipped kitchen, kitchen pantry, and butler's pantry, plus dining rooms and breakfast rooms/conservatories.

Riordan State Historic Park is open year around, except Christmas Day.

Salade Verte et Rouge

*The Whitwell Hospital at First and Adams in Tucson adver-
tised its culinary service in the early 1900s as unusually excellent. "The poorest and most jaded invalid appetites are tempt-
ed by the dainty trays prepared in our diet kitchen," read one
pamphlet, complete with recipes. This lettuce and ham salad
convinced me that Dr. Hobart Shattuck, Physician-in-Charge,
was ahead of his time.*

"Take 3 heads of cabbage lettuce, strip off all the white
leaves, put them in ice cold water, reserve the hearts. Cut the
cold ham into thin, even slices, and lay over-lapping on a
piece of carefully trimmed bread placed in the center of a
platter. Around this place the lettuce leaves, which must be
carefully drained by putting them on a clean napkin and shaking it well, taking care not to bruise them, as they lose their
taste if not crisp. Cut each of the lettuce hearts into 4 pieces
and slice a couple of hard-boiled eggs. These can be kept
from crumbling by taking care to cook them only 7 minutes
in boiling water. Just before the salad is to be served, a por-
tion of the French Dressing, prepared fresh meantime, should
be poured gently over the lettuce leaves. Then place over
them the sliced hearts, with a slice of egg between each. Pour
over these the remainder of the dressing and serve quickly.

"French Dressing: this is made by putting 6 tablespoons of
good olive oil in a bowl, adding 1 coffee spoonful of salt, 1
salt spoonful of pepper, 2 tablespoonfuls of tarragon vinegar.
Beat them together until smooth with a silver fork."

French Dressing
6 tablespoons olive oil
1 coffee spoonful of salt
1 salt spoonful of pepper
2 tablespoons tarragon vinegar

Sheepherder's Salad

*Sheepherder's Salad originated with camp cooking where
greens were not readily available. A can of tomatoes was
always in the chuck box and onions, cucumbers, and bell
peppers travel better than lettuce and such. Something fresh
was a must.*

Clean vegetables and peel, chop, or slice. Mix and toss
everything in one big bowl or tub. Serves 15 with starvation
appetites. No need to chill. That's the idea behind this salad,
given to me by Truman McDaniel, camp cook.

4 large onions, peeled and chopped
2 bunches green onions, chopped with tops
2 or 3 bell peppers, seeded and sliced
3 cucumbers, sliced thin, unpeeled
4 cans tomatoes, 16-ounce
7 or 8 tablespoons sugar
1 tablespoon each, salt and pepper

Aspic

An admirable aspic before gelatin was perfected had to be a labor of love. Veal knuckles and calves' feet were boiled for as much as seven hours and allowed to "sweat" over a stove; when the resulting herbed consomme was strained through a napkin, the cook had calves' foot jelly or aspic. This was combined with incredible ingredients, such as cocks' combs, calf brains (using both ends of the calf), and sweetbreads. The flossier forts and fashionable communities in Arizona used aspics as part of their midnight suppers after dances. I suspect most men detested them. The Settlement Cook Book of 1921 was used by Eleanor Sloan, the daughter of Territorial Governor Richard Sloan. She used this recipe straight from the book during the aspic's heyday before World War II.

2 tablespoons gelatin
juice of 1 lemon
2 cups boiling water
1 teaspoon salt
½ cup sugar
¼ cup vinegar
3 cups diced celery, red peppers, and olives
1 cup boiled shrimp or crab, optional

Soak gelatin in 1 cup cold water 5 minutes. Add boiling water, stir until dissolved. Add lemon juice, salt, sugar, and vinegar. Stir well, set aside, and when aspic begins to set, add 3 cups of any of the ingredients listed. Turn into mold and chill. Serve with mayonnaise dressing.

My great Aunt Maude went to Fanny Farmer Cooking School in Boston to learn to make perfect aspics, but I took her Maple Syrup Mousse over Tomato Aspic any day.

Arizona Fruit Plate

A favorite of Mrs. Carl Hayden, all ingredients being Arizona-produced.

First, chill plate thoroughly. Have lettuce leaves well-chilled to arrange on plates. Then cut 3-inch square of watermelon, then 3-inch oblong of honeydew melon, half a peach, 1 peeled ripe fig, and 2 tablespoons of cottage cheese. Place cottage cheese on center of plate. Place fruit around cheese. Then place 3 strawberries on top of cheese. Salad dressing or whipped cream could be used to garnish.

Wilted Greens

From fresh watercress to early dandelion and other weed greens, a dishpan or bucket brimming full meant tangy wilted salad or greens coming up. Mrs. J. J. (Alice) Reese of Navajo tossed her greens together this way.

Gather, wash, and pat dry 1 quart greens. Fry bacon until crisp. Add vinegar and water. Heat. Combine greens, onions, seasoning, and sugar, if desired. Pour hot mixture over greens; toss until wilted. Best with corn bread.

watercress, lettuce, or available greens
4 slices bacon, cut up
¼ cup vinegar
2 tablespoons water
2 green onions, chopped
salt and pepper to taste
1 teaspoon sugar, optional

Down the Colorado with Major Powell

"1869. John Wesley Powell and his men had been on the river since May 4. They had lost most of their supplies. Their clothes were soaked; so, too, was their food. Flour and coffee were like mush from constant wetting. The bacon was gritty and the beans were sprouting. The canyon walls shut them too tightly for hunting trips except for an occasional duck or goose and a few fish. They longed for greens.

"On July 6, on an island near the mouth of the White River they came upon a small garden patch, planted and then abandoned by a passing trapper; and though there were no ripe vegetables to be found, there were plenty of green potato-tops, and these they cooked into what they hoped would be a nourishing stew. Soon, every man jack of them was clutching his stomach, then rolling on the ground with cramps. And even when they at last got going, they were so weak from vomiting that they could scarcely lift their sweep and oars.

" 'Potato tops,' Jack Sumner noted in his diary, 'are not good greens on the sixth day of July.' "

James Russey Ullman, Riverside Press.

Fried Green Chiles

The Hopi Indian Reservation spreads out over three mesas between the San Francisco Peaks and the Lukachukai Mountains. Hopi ancestors were among the earliest people to settle the Southwest, and most Hopis still live on the mesas in what appear to be the area's first condominiums. A few have ranches on the plateaus where they skillfully farm fruits, grains, and vegetables. Chiles are grown in the terrace gardens below First Mesa, watered by abundant springs. My Hopi friend, Inez Tewawina, explained to me that women inherit garden space from their mothers and plant chile peppers as a staple. They string them to dry and grind their own chile powder, keeping a little bowl on the dining table. Inez's favorite vegetable was fried chile—crisp-cooked like Chinese vegetables.

12 fresh green chile pods
4 tablespoons salt pork drippings

Use the freshest green chiles possible. Wash and clean, removing the stems, but not the seeds. Cut a little slot in each side which lets the steam out while they are frying. If you forget, the chiles will spatter while they brown. Heat about 2 tablespoons of salt pork drippings in a frying pan and put a few green chiles at a time into pan. Stand there and keep turning. Make sure chiles are lightly browned. They are just right when the top part gets brown but the inside is still green. Add shortening as needed to complete cooking. Eat hot or cold, allowing 2 per person.

Chinle Creamed Onions

Thunderbird Lodge, made a legend of Canyon de Chelly by Leon (Cozy) McSparron and his wife, Inja, was a place for observing a Navajo trading post, listening to history, and dining with the family. Pot roast and creamed onions and Cozy's stories brought guests back for more. This exceptional trader is responsible for the Chinle-style Navajo rug. His wife was responsible for the onions, a dish historically served by pioneer cooks on winter holidays.

12 small to medium onions
¼ cup butter
1 cup white sauce
1 cup table cream
¼ teaspoon nutmeg
⅓ cup onion broth
1 pinch sugar
salt and pepper to taste

Steam cleaned onions in water to cover, slightly salted, until tender. Drain and save broth. Melt butter in a heavy saucepan, add white sauce, cream, onion broth, and seasonings. Mrs. McSparron added fresh parsley when available. Stir until mixture begins to boil. Add onions and simmer until heated through. These may be put in oven-proof dish and kept in oven until serving time.

Basic Beans

In Come an' Get It, *the story of the old cowboy cook, Ramon F. Adams commented that beans were such a staple in cattle country that meal time was referred to as "bean time" on many parts of the range. Mostly, they were called "free-holes." The 1909* Mission Cook Book *of Tucson bears him out, with this recipe.*

Frijoles (Spanish Beans)—Use the red or Spanish beans. Boil a cupful until soft, several hours before using, setting them aside to cool in the water they were boiled in. Put a tablespoon of sweet oil or very nice dripping into a frying pan. Add a small chopped onion and before it browns, add the beans with some of the water in which they were boiled. Season liberally with finely chopped chile peppers and salt. Eat in bowls or mash them as they cook. Can be served at any meal.

The common camp and kitchen recipe is just as valid today as when Tex Taylor sang:

"The pinto bean is hard to beat, with dry salt in the pot. Frijoles? Well it's jes' the same, jes' give me what y'u've got."

2 cups pinto beans, soaked overnight
¼ pound or more salt pork
2 quarts water
1 or 2 cloves garlic
salt and pepper

Scholey Beans
(Best Darn Beans in the State)

Charley Scholey owned a Prescott pool hall. His wife made these beans every day and every day for years; they sold every bean.

Wash and clean beans. Soak overnight in warm water, no salt. Add pork, onion, and lard, and cook until beans get tender. Cook red chiles in small amount of water until tender. Work through a colander. Fry round steak in its own suet. When well done, put through meat grinder. Add garlic, red and green chiles, ground meat to the beans. Cook over low heat long enough to mingle all flavors.

1 quart dried red beans
½ pound salt pork
1 large onion, cut up fine
1 cup lard or other cooking fat
several dried red Mexican chile peppers
½ pound round steak
1 can green chiles or 3 fresh fried chiles
1 clove garlic
salt to taste

Frijoles Borrachos

These "slightly drunken beans" are cooked basically like most pinto beans. They contain no meat, but two cloves of garlic and one bottle of beer seem to make up very nicely for the lack of salt pork or beef. This was given to me by Mrs. Norman Williams, wife of the genial Mexican consul.

Cook cleaned beans with water until they boil up. Remove from heat and cover 2 hours. Add remaining ingredients and bring to a boil again. Lower the heat to simmer and cover and cook from 4 to 6 hours until tender but not mushy. Taste about a half-hour before serving time. If salt is needed, add then but not before. Salt hardens beans when added too soon. Serves 6 to 8 with warm flour tortillas.

1 pound pinto beans, cleaned
6 cups water
4 tomatoes, chopped
5 diced chiles
2 cloves garlic, diced
1 onion, diced
1 bottle beer of choice, preferably Mexican

Fruits and vegetables came straight from the home garden to the dinner table, but these were good enough to take a detour to the Yavapai County Fair in the 1920s. Photo displays bragged about the produce of Little Chino Valley, north of Prescott. SHARLOT HALL MUSEUM

Scalloped Tomatoes

Many vegetables were scalloped, which meant they were combined with cheese or milk and dotted with butter and baked. This recipe comes from Butterick's Correct Cookery, *an old cookbook cherished by Lois Garver Soderman, an Arizona native. Her mother used it often, and the family appreciated it almost as much as the Capitol Street Car Line of Phoenix, which was installed by Lois' engineer grandfather, G.R. Sturdevant.*

fresh tomatoes
boiling water
cold water
salt and pepper
bread crumbs
fresh butter
grated cheese

Skin several fresh tomatoes by dropping in boiling water for 1 minute, then plunging into cold water. Skins slip off and stem ends can be removed with a knife. Slice ½ inch thick and place a layer in a bacon-greased baking dish. Add a light seasoning of salt and pepper; then a thick layer of crumbs. Cut a teaspoon of butter into tiny pieces and place on bread crumbs. Sprinkle with cheese. Repeat until sufficient quantity has been prepared. Bake about 30 minutes at 350 degrees. Bacon or leftover chopped meat may be added to make this a main dish.

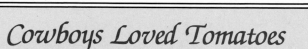

Cowboys Loved Tomatoes

The cowman did not seem to relish such vegetables as canned corn, peas, and their like. Canned tomatoes, on the other hand, filled a large place in his cravings. While he knew nothing of the vitamin content advertised today, there was that tangy acidity his system seemed to demand. And since canned tomatoes were cheap, the boss could afford to keep a good supply on hand.

"Tomatoes served as a food but were most satisfying as a thirst quencher, allaying thirst even longer than water. A man going on a dry ride would likely take a can or two of tomatoes along; also a man coming in from such a ride would go to the wagon and open a can of tomatoes to cut the dust and thirst.

"No cowhand liked to 'pack' a lunch, so line riders and fence riders often carried only a can or two of tomatoes rolled in their slickers to serve as food and drink. If drinking water was poor, he preferred tomatoes to a canteen.

"Tomatoes stewed with a little sugar and leftover biscuits made a tasty dish. Some enjoyed it as much as they did dessert.

"For no reason, this dish was known as 'pooch.' Besides tomatoes and canned milk, few canned goods were carried with the chuckwagon."

Ramon F. Adams in *Come an' Get It.*

Kruse Carrots

Dorothy and Fred Kruse were both German-born. They met in California and married, homesteading in Casa Grande, Arizona, but settling near Phoenix, by the old Yuma Trail (now Van Buren) and Lateral 18. Their family of eleven helped make the farm successful, picking and tying and helping sell onions, bell peppers, eggplant, okra, beets, turnips, corn, beans, melons, and carrots. Fred Kruse was president of the Maricopa County Farmer's Union when Bartlett Dam was dedicated. This recipe made the carrots disappear.

Clean and shred carrots. Cut apricots into fine strips. Heat butter and water in large skillet over medium heat. Add carrots, then apricots. Sauté 2 or 3 minutes. Sprinkle sugar over the top. Add vinegar. Stir and cook rapidly until nicely glazed, about 1 minute. Serve at once.

1 pound carrots, shredded
6 dried apricots
2 tablespoons butter
2 tablespoons water
1 tablespoon sugar
1 tablespoon good wine vinegar

Ranching always meant more than just cattle. The Clough Ranch near Prescott, about 1900, included orchards and vineyards against a colorful backdrop of granite outcroppings. SHARLOT HALL MUSEUM

Jewel's Squash

Arizona's third territorial governor, A. P. K. Safford, named Florence, Arizona, after his sister. In 1903, it was predicted that Florence would be the mining and agricultural center of the West. Because of water problems, Florence stayed a small city on the south bank of the Gila River. Yet it became the site of the Arizona State Prison in 1909, and four years later Bill and Mark Twain Clemans set up what became the largest cattle outfit in Pinal County. Jewel (Mrs. W. J. Clemans Sr.) was a noted hostess, using this recipe for squash, artichokes, onions, or string beans!

Cut squash in half and steam until tender. Remove squash centers into bowl. Place shells in bottom of well-oiled baking dish. Squeeze water out of squash centers. Mix pulp with powdered crackers and add cheese, parsley, garlic, herbs, nutmeg, salt, pepper, and olive oil. Spread this mixture over shells. Beat eggs to a froth. Spoon over shells with a little cheese and a dash of nutmeg as topping. Bake until set in slow oven, 325 degrees. Do not overcook. Serve hot or cold. Can be made in pie plate with onions, string beans, or artichokes.

6 small zucchini squash
3 eggs
3 soda crackers, powdered
1 cup grated Italian cheese
chopped parsley
2 cloves garlic
dash of herbs, your choice
salt and pepper to taste
¼ teaspoon nutmeg
2 teaspoons olive oil

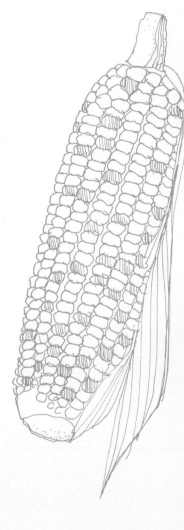

Hopi Sprouts and Corn

Beans have great ritual significance to the Hopi. They are sprouted in the winter in the Kivas before the Powamu or bean ceremony and dance. Sprouts and corn go into a ceremonial dish like this, which formerly was only made in February at bean dance time. Now that sprouts are on sale at some markets, the dish is made more often in town, for potlucks and church suppers.

Clean, wash, and rinse one small basket of sprouts. Put them in a big kettle with water and salt and bring to a boil. Cook at least 2 hours. Shell some ears of white dried Hopi corn. Wash it and boil in another pan. When corn pops open, it is done. Cut up a chunk of salt pork and sauté it in a heavy pan. Put meat, and drippings, corn, and some of the corn liquid into the boiling sprouts. Cook another hour so the flavors blend. Serve.

That's How Dad Saw It

Honest John Anderson came to the Phoenix area as a retired executive and possum chef, born in the deep South. His daddy gave him a rating system for vegetables.

Artichokes are much work; leeks are an onion designed by a committee; parsnips are nature's mistake, and squash is simply squish.

When his mother asked his father if he'd consider eating broccoli or cauliflower, dear old dad said very quietly, "I not only would not eat it, my dear; I wouldn't even step on it."

An herb garden was a serious matter for ranch wives who set a good table for family as well as guests. Adeline Hall cuts dill from her garden on the Orchard Ranch near Prescott, about 1907. SHARLOT HALL MUSEUM

Pan Fried Apples, 1919

Two heroines of Zane Grey novels taught me how to fry apples over an open fire in Star Valley. Myrtle Haught Branstetter, whom Grey used as a prototype for Rose of the Tonto, *and her sister, Arllie Haught Ezell, the little girl of several Tonto Rim books, have warm memories of the days their father, Anderson Lee (Babe) Haught, guided hunting and fishing parties in Rim territory. Pan-Fried Apples or a cobbler topped off campfire dinners to perfection.*

Heat apple slices in hot bacon drippings until they soften, stirring to turn over. Add honey or brown sugar and a little salt and cinnamon, if available. If not, honey or sugar will glaze the slices if allowed to remain on the fire, covered, 5 to 10 minutes, depending on heat. These make a great camp meal anywhere, even at the backyard barbecue.

3 or 4 large, tart apples, cored and sliced
2 tablespoons bacon drippings or butter
1/3 cup wild bee honey or brown sugar
salt and cinnamon

Annie's Baked Apples and Apple Butter

Genevieve Sparks grew up in Prescott, the daughter of Dr. John Bryan and Annie Sweeney McNally. Genevieve's husband and son died as they slept when the house caught fire a night before Christmas. She moved to Wickenburg and became everybody's favorite first grade teacher until she retired. She told me her mother made magic with apples and gave me the proof of it.

Baked Apples: Pare and core 6 tart apples of equal size. Arrange in a baking dish. Place a teaspoon of sugar or honey in each hollow and add a spoon of raisins or currants. Sprinkle with cinnamon and a bit of orange peel, if available. After they begin to bake in hot oven, baste with a scant half-cup of water in which 2 spoons of butter have been melted. Baste 3 times, after which the apples should be done. Serve hot for breakfast or a winter supper with a dusting of sugar and a splash of cream.

Baked Apple Butter: Pare and quarter apples to cook in large kettle to make 9 cups applesauce. Into large baking pan, spread applesauce mixed with 5 cups sugar, ½ cup apple cider vinegar, 1 teaspoon allspice, ½ teaspoon ground cloves, and ½ teaspoon cinnamon. Bake 3 hours in 350-degree oven, stirring every half hour. Sterilize 5 pint jars and drain. Add the Apple Butter to within inch of the top, filling while very hot and sealing at once. Magic for sure with freshly baked bread.

6 tart apples
6 teaspoons sugar or honey
1 teaspoon raisins or currants
cinnamon
orange peel
½ cup water
2 teaspoons melted butter
Baked Apple Butter
9 cups applesauce
5 cups of sugar
½ cup apple cider vinegar
1 teaspoon allspice
½ teaspoon ground cloves
½ teaspoon cinnamon

Sauerkraut in Jars

Sauerkraut was made in tubs, crocks, and glass jars but never in a metal container. Lois Plummer Stone told fellow members of the Auxiliary to the Arizona Museum how her Arizona pioneer parents made this hearty, inexpensive (although smelly) dish. Cabbage was a most successful crop here.

5 pounds mature cabbage
3½ tablespoons salt
cold water

Remove outer leaves and cut clean cabbage very fine. Mix well with salt. Pack firmly into clean sterile jars. Fill jars with cold water. Be sure water goes to the bottom of the jars. Remove any air bubbles by inserting a knife where you can see bubbles in jars. Put on cap and screw the band tight. Kraut will ferment in 4 or 5 days. (We kept ours behind a wood stove, which certainly made for an odoriferous kitchen.) When fermentation is over, wash jars, tighten bands, and store without processing. Will be ready to cook with pork or hot dogs in 6 to 8 weeks. This keeps for many months in a cool place—not behind the stove.

From Old Cookbooks

of the Grandview Women's Club in Phoenix (no longer in existence)

Herbs—They should be gathered when just beginning to blossom as they are then in their perfection. Medicinal herbs should be dried, put up in paper bags, and labeled. Cooking herbs should be pounded, sifted, put into bottles or boxes and labeled. Herbs retain their virtue best dried by artificial heat. The warmth of an oven a few hours after the bread is drawn is sufficient.

***

He is a sorry cook who cannot lick his own fingers. (1880 cookbook)

***

Substitute for coffee: Scrape clean 3 or 4 good parsnips, cut them into thin slices, bake till well brown in low oven, grind or crush and use in the same manner as coffee, from which it is scarcely distinguishable. This is not only a beverage equally good as coffee but it is likewise a cure for asthma.

***

Dead fish and daughters are not keeping wares. (1880 cookbook)

***

Tainted Meat: Tainted meat may be rendered good by pickling it in potash water for some time. Before it is cooked, however, it should be dipped in vinegar for a short while and then salted in brine.

Chapter 9

Cheese and Churn: The Way It Was

According to Bob Reidy, historian for the United Dairymen of Arizona, "We had a dairy industry and a beef industry when the Pilgrims landed. Almost anyone who migrated to the Phoenix area brought or bought a cow."

The Spanish introduced chickens, eggs as a natural result, milk cattle, and citrus to the territory. The cow and the hen became a daily part of most women's lives.

The Diary of Lucy Hannah Flake (1896) set down her morning chores. "Get up, turn out my chickkens, draw a pail of water, water garden beds, make a fire, put potatoes on to cook, brush and sweep half an inch of dust off floor and everything, feed three litters of chickkens, then mix bisquits, milk the cows and this morning go half-mile after calves."

Milk became butter and cheese and buttermilk for enriching the family, the stock, and the baked goods. The Mormon way of building a fortress provided a safeguard for their dairy needs. At Pipe Spring National Monument today, docents make butter and cheese in the traditional setting.

The Gear family established the Central Avenue Dairy in Phoenix in 1897, and the nearby Laveen area became an early dairy showplace of the state, thanks to Armon D. Cheatham; his father, William C., and his brother, Shelton. The family sold their dairy in Duncan to move to Laveen in 1919. Eventually, with the help of Armon's four sons, they owned the largest registered Holstein herd in the United States, milking in excess of 500 head a day, seven days a week.

State growth expanded the industry to 155 dairies with an average of 550 cows each. Every town had a milkman who brought your order to the doorstep. The emergence of big markets and availability of the family car brought about the demise of home delivery and the wonderful way it was.

The free-flowing water at Pipe Spring was a natural focal point for explorers, travelers, and settlers in the vast, arid Arizona Strip. Mormon missionaries, Dr. James M. Whitmore, former Texas cattleman and his herder, Robert McIntyre, settled this area in 1863. Both were killed by marauding Indians less than three years later.

A sort of peace came to the Arizona Strip when the Utah Militia garrisoned Pipe Spring in 1868.

Meanwhile, Mormon leader Brigham Young became interested in Pipe Spring as the location for a tithing herd—the cattle contributed by church members as a tenth of their income. Construction of a fort was begun by Joseph W. Young, and completed under the supervision of Anson P. Winsor. Named for the man who operated the ranch for the church, Winsor Castle consists of two rectangular, two-story houses, with walls extended to form a courtyard. Smaller buildings housed church members who worked on the fort.

A large herd was built up, and soon Pipe Spring produced cheese, butter, and beef. Some went to St. George, Utah, for the workers building the Mormon Temple there; the rest was marketed elsewhere.

When the fort was in its heyday, part of the spring was diverted directly into a spring room, where the constant water temperature of fifty-six degrees was helpful in curing cheese. Production of cheese was about sixty to eighty pounds a day.

Pipe Spring National Monument is open all year, except for Thanksgiving, Christmas and New Year's Day. Costumed guides demonstrate pioneer activities such as rug weaving, quilting, baking, candle dipping, soap making, cheese making, and butter churning.

Butter

No branch of household economy brings better reward than the making of butter. The first requisite is to have a good cow. Have her milked by a person who understands the process or she will not give it freely and will soon become dry. Strain the milk as soon as it is brought into the house and set it quickly in the milk room. The custom of churning once a week is not to be tolerated. Cream that is kept seven days, unless it be in the coldest weather, cannot be made into good butter. Churn in the cool of the morning. If the weather is warm, set the churn in a tub of cold water; add ice if you have it. When the butter has come, continue the strokes of the dasher a few minutes to separate all the little particles from the buttermilk.

Doris Heath's *Cracker Barrel Cook Book*, compiled from early settler cookbooks

Old-Time Cottage Cheese

Place milk in several pans to clabber. (Clabber is to settle into a sour, smooth state.) After clabbering, place in a large flat-bottomed kettle. Place the kettle on the stove on low heat and do not let the milk simmer or boil. While the milk is heating slowly, cut through the clabbered milk cross-wise with a knife to separate the curds and let the milk heat evenly. When the curds of milk and the whey have separated (the thin whey will come to the top) take a clean old pillowcase or salt bag and pour the mixture into it. When it is all in the bag, squeeze lightly and hang on the clothesline with it pinned at the top and let it hang overnight. The next morning bring in the bag and make your cottage cheese. Salt and pepper to taste, and then add just enough sweet or sour cream to coat the dry curds. If you like, you can add a pinch of chives or sage or both.

From Bertha Barnes' *Antique Cookbook*

(RIGHT) The diligent housewife churned butter daily, usually in the cool morning. Possibly wearing her Sunday apron, a Yavapai County ranch matriarch shows how the job was done, about 1900. SHARLOT HALL MUSEUM

English Monkey

Charles and Harriet Ann Hirst came to Glendale in 1892, where he managed the Ranch of the Fig until floods, then drought, wiped out the trees. For fifteen years he managed the extensive real estate holdings of Dwight B. Heard and helped organize the Salt River Valley Water Users Association. Charles built a solar system for the family's hot water. He liked to cook fried tomato gravy for breakfast, a dish little known now. He peeled and sliced tomatoes, rolled them in flour, browned them in butter, then added cream and served them on toast. His wife's favorite dish was from her British background, resembling a souffle, but with never a fall.

Grate the three cheeses and mix with bread crumbs. Beat eggs, then beat in milk and butter. When frothy, add all other ingredients. Bake at 350 about 45 minutes until firm and set. This will bake faster in a flat pan.

1 pound grated cheeses, sharp, cheddar, and longhorn
1 cup bread crumbs
4 eggs
1½ cups milk
2 tablespoons clarified butter
½ teaspoon dry mustard
1 teaspoon salt
⅛ teaspoon cayenne pepper
½ teaspoon paprika

The wooden lookout tower atop Winsor Castle at Pipe Spring is a reminder that the sandstone-block structure originally was a fort. The wall and gate enclosing the courtyard had been removed by 1887, when residents gathered for this photograph.
NATIONAL PARK SERVICE.

Cheese Grits

Grits, often called hominy grits, are finely ground, dry hulled corn kernels. A side of grits is considered a taste of heaven in the South and the feeling came into the Southwest with loyal pioneers. Adding cheese, eggs, and butter converted many who never imagined lowly grits could be dinner party fare. Mary Favour Hazeltine, wife of Sherman, longtime president of the First National Bank of Arizona, called this a grits souffle.

Cook water, grits, and salt in double boiler until smooth and thick. Stir as it bubbles. Combine remaining ingredients with cooked grits. Use thyme, rosemary, lemon pepper, or any combination of herbs, if desired. Bake in buttered casserole at 325 degrees about 40 minutes—until silver knife inserted into center comes out clean. Holds indefinitely in warm oven.

6 cups water
1½ cups grits
2 teaspoons salt
favorite herbs
1 pound grated cheese
3 large eggs, beaten
½ cup butter
dash of Tabasco sauce

Macaroni and Cheese

The great Depression answer to what's-for-dinner was filling and familiar macaroni, baked with cheese—sometimes in white sauce and sometimes in a light egg custard. My husband's mother put bread crumbs on top; my mother added one-half cup of leftover smoked ham. Some cooks added tuna or salmon. This is the basic. It was a popular winter dish baked in the same oven with a crusty meat loaf.

Cook macaroni in boiling salted water to cover in uncovered saucepan until tender, about 9 minutes. Drain and pour cold water through macaroni. Put into buttered baking dish. Add butter, coarsely grated cheese. Rat cheese was store cheese, the kind the grocer had under a big glass cover to cut on order. Cheddar or American would do but rat cheese had good sharp flavor. Heat milk and add seasonings. Beat eggs to a slight foam and add hot, seasoned milk. Stir and pour over macaroni and cheese. Bake, uncovered, at 350 degrees for 45 minutes.

1½ cups elbow macaroni
boiling salted water
¼ cup water
½ pound rat cheese
1 tablespoon parsley
2 cups milk
⅛ teaspoon pepper
½ teaspoon salt
½ teaspoon paprika
2 eggs

Pasqua Cheese

Easter at Frank Lloyd Wright's Taliesin West near Scottsdale became a festival of friendship and Old World food because of his hospitable wife, Olgivanna. She grew up in Montenegro in Yugoslavia on the Adriatic Sea, where the Greek Orthodox Church richly celebrated Easter. Baba, a velvety egg bread like no other, was baked in buttered rounds of paper, then gently rocked on pillows until cool. Pasqua or Pashka (from the Greek word pasha, meaning to pass over) is a creamy almond and raisin cheese to spread on the Baba. Over a thousand eggs were boiled and hand painted or dyed for guests, staff, and students. Although the Wrights are deceased, Taliesen Easter goes on. This recipe, very similar to the old family version, has been reduced for home use.

Press any excess moisture from cheese. Blend with sour cream, softened butter, salt, sugar, and vanilla. Add finely grated lemon rind, finely ground or chopped almonds, and the raisins. When the mixture is very smooth, place in a muslin or napkin-lined receptacle (traditionally cone-shaped), which will allow the mixture to drain. Put weight on top and store in a cool place. To serve, turn out on a dish or bowl and decorate with fresh berries or fruit.

3 pounds cottage cheese
½ cup sour cream
¼ pound soft butter
1 teaspoon salt
⅔ cup sugar
1 teaspoon vanilla
2 tablespoons grated lemon rind
2 ounces finely ground almonds
5 tablespoons seedless raisins
fresh berries or candied fruit

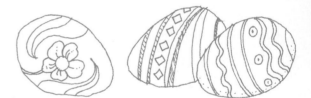

Oven Eggs
(A Good Lenten Dish)

There was a time when almost every cook knew how to make a white sauce or a cream sauce (for the fearless), and during Lent, or after Easter when hard-boiled eggs had lost their holiday charm, this dish emerged. Barbara Trask, a faithful Pink Lady volunteer at Good Samaritan Hospital in Phoenix, revived her eggs with Tabasco.

Mix milk, cream, melted butter, salt, cayenne, and Tabasco and blend very well. Cook in top of double boiler, stirring constantly, until smooth and thickened. In a well-buttered 2-quart casserole, place a thin layer of cracker crumbs. Cover with a thin layer of cream sauce; top with a layer of cheese, then a sprinkling of pimentos, then eggs. Continue in layers, ending with crumbs on top. You can mix ¼ cup crumbs and ¼ cup cheese for topping. Dot with butter. Bake in 350-degree oven 30 to 40 minutes, or until bubbling and top is brown. Do not cook too stiff; it should be a little creamy. Serve with green peas or broccoli for color.

1 cup milk
1 cup cream
¼ cup melted butter
½ teaspoon salt
dash of cayenne pepper
dash of Tabasco sauce
1 cup cracker crumbs
2 cups shredded cheese
4 canned pimentos, sliced
4 hard-cooked eggs, sliced
2 tablespoons butter

Lucy's Goldenrod Eggs

Teachers in early Arizona were smothered in regulations. They could not loiter in an ice cream parlor and were not supposed to "keep company with men." At one time, they had to wear two petticoats. Even so, when Lucy (Mrs. Edward Carl) Spangler arrived in Bisbee to teach, her dance card was filled out for the entire year within a week. "How I got Carl, I'll never be sure," she commented. "The only recipe I knew was for Goldenrod Eggs." This recipe was a must for young ladies.

Separate yolk and white of egg and chop whites. Put the yolks in a warm place. Melt butter in a saucepan. Remove from fire and mix with flour and seasonings. Cook until it bubbles, then add milk gradually, stirring constantly until smooth. Add the chopped whites to the sauce. Heat throughly and stir, then pour over hot toast. Press the yolks over the whole, through a fine strainer. Garnish with toast points and parsley and serve at once.

4 hard-cooked eggs
2 tablespoons butter
2 tablespoons flour
salt and pepper to taste
¼ teaspoon nutmeg, optional
1 cup hot milk
6 to 8 slices toast
fresh parsley

Swiss Quiche

Long before Quiche Lorraine became an American fad food, it was a European specialty, zesty with cayenne-tinged cream and Swiss cheese. Elizabeth Homrighausien, who began dairy operations in Phoenix in 1914, also taught at Phoenix Union High School and promoted 4-H projects. Production from her purebred Holstein herd was just what this recipe needed, in a pre-calorie-counting era.

Fry bacon slowly until crisp. Drain well and blot with paper towels. Break into small pieces. Beat eggs and cream until thick. Add seasonings. Rub pie shell with softened butter. Sprinkle bacon and grated cheese on bottom of the shell. Pour custard mixture over bacon and cheese. Bake at 425 degrees 15 minutes. Reduce oven temperature to 300 degrees and bake 30 minutes. Bring out of oven with care and let stand out of drafts for 5 minutes before serving.

12 slices bacon
4 eggs
2 cups heavy cream
¾ teaspoon salt
pinch of nutmeg
pinch of sugar
pinch of cayenne pepper
2 tablespoons soft butter
¼ pound Swiss cheese, grated
unbaked 9-inch pie shell

Chapter 10
Wood Stove Sweets

Arizona desserts began with wild honey and fruit, baked agave, and husk-wrapped corn pudding. Even earliest man seemed to yearn for a touch of something sweet.

Pima Historian Anna Shaw wrote: "Huge storage baskets were filled with saguaro syrup, cholla fruit, mesquite cakes, melon strips, and there was honey, too." The sweet tooth has been with us in Arizona as far as we can trace.

The padres knew the hunger well. They ordered large amounts of chocolate when supply lists went to Spain. Wine was ordered before the grapes were planted, and they never ordered less than an arroba (twenty-five pounds) of sugar.

Fort and chuck wagon cooks were valued for their desserts, with pie as traditional a food as beef and beans. Butterfield stations on the Overland Route soothed dusty passengers with corn cakes or apple pie. Fresh apples, dried apples, pan-fried apples, or applesauce sent many a pioneer to a hard bed with a soft smile.

Cake baking became an art according to every old cookbook, whether compiled by church groups or Army wives. Because good baking began with chopped wood, properly laid, baking was an exercise both physical and mathematical. The hand which judged the oven ruled the roost.

Our range history developed the most colorful dessert cooks of all, with language to match. Doughnuts were "bear sign." Rice pudding with raisins was "spotted pup." Pancakes were "saddle blankets." Molasses sweetened most desserts, affectionately dubbed "lick" or "larrup." Ramon F. Adams reported: "A cowboy would go to hell for a piece of pie."

Ranch "fluff duffs" became more elegant in town when mining and railroads added a touch of glamour. Champagne pie crust and whiskey cake reached their heights when gold and silver were being mined at a reckless rate.

Woman decided no main meal was complete without dessert. Sometimes dessert *was* the meal. Early summer dinners consisted of soup plates filled with tenderly crusted shortcake, heaped with fresh strawberries, topped with sugar, and milk fresh from the cow. Fall suppers were sometimes apples dumpled in burnished pastry, steaming of cinnamon and sugar, and again topped with milk or cream. Getting your calcium was heaven.

Built in 1895 for Dr. and Mrs. Roland Lee Rosson at a cost of $7,525, Rosson House is an outstanding example of the Victorian Eastlake style so popular in San Francisco in the late 1800s.

Phoenix was one-quarter century old. The city of 10,000 people was experiencing its first building boom. Many of the newcomers were from the Midwest and tried to re-create the homes and gardens typical of that part of the country.

Dr. Rosson became the Mayor of Phoenix soon after moving into his new home. Rosson House was one of the most prominent homes in town. The expansive veranda had lattice-like ornamentation of lathe-worked posts and smaller spindles. First and second-story windows were paired, and the third story featured an octagonal turret with elaborate finial and spool-like ornamentation. The interior consisted of ten rooms. Notable were the pressed-tin ceilings, elaborately carved staircase, and parquet floors inlaid with oak, walnut, and mahogany.

The property changed hands many times, and when the city embarked on its first major historical restoration project in 1974, it purchased Rosson House for $80,000. Rosson House is located at Heritage Square, the only remaining group of residential structures in the original townsite of Phoenix. The kitchen is a model of the well-appointed turn-of-the century household.

Lady Baltimore Cake

Mrs. William H. Sawtelle and Mrs. Harry R. Webber, Tucson matrons, made difficult cakes sound simple with their short recipes: no specific temperatures and no-nonsense instructions. A good cook KNOWS these things.

"One cupful of butter, two cupfuls of sugar, three and one-half cupfuls of flour, one cupful of sweet milk, the whites of six eggs, two level teaspoonful of baking powder and one teaspoonful of rose water. Cream butter; add sugar gradually, beating continuously; then the milk and the flavoring, next the flour into which the baking powder has been sifted, and lastly the beaten whites which should be folded in lightly. Bake in three layer cake pans in an oven that is hotter than it would be for loaf cake.

"Filling: Dissolve three cupfuls of sugar in one cup of boiling water. Cook until it threads; pour it over stiffly beaten whites of three eggs, beating constantly. To this add one cup chopped raisins, one cup chopped nutmeats and a half-dozen figs cut in very thin strips. This will fill between layers, sides and top."   Mrs. WHS.

1 cup butter
2 cups sugar
3½ cups flour
1 cup sweet milk
6 egg whites
2 teaspoons baking powder

Filling
3 cups sugar
1 cup boiling water
3 egg whites
1 cup chopped raisins
1 cup chopped nutmeats
6 figs, cut in strips

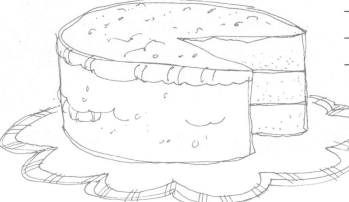

Mahogany Cake

"One-quarter cake of chocolate cooked in a half cupful of milk. Let stand until cold. One and one-half cups brown sugar, one-half cup sour milk, one teaspoon soda, one teaspoon vanilla, two cups flour. Bake in loaf or layers." Mrs. HRW.

From *The Bazar Cook Book*, 1909, Tucson.

¼ cake chocolate
½ cup milk
½ cup brown sugar
½ cup sour milk
1 teaspoon soda
1 teaspoon vanilla
2 cups flour

The Family Birthday Cake

Evo DeConcini's father brought his family to Tucson in 1921. Evo, who became a justice of the Arizona Supreme Court, married Ora Damron Webster, a native of Central in Graham County. Their family of four prized a cinnamon chocolate cake which Ora tried during a national contest for naming the cake. "The prize was $25,000, and I never found out who won and with what name." she said. "But our family has probably used this recipe 25,000 times." Son Dennis, who became a U.S. Senator, calls this the Family Birthday Cake— name enough.

Sift sugar and cream with shortening until light and thoroughly mixed. Add well-beaten eggs. Sift flour once before measuring, then sift with dry ingredients. Add to creamed batter alternately with sour buttermilk. Add flavorings and nuts. Pour into well-greased and floured layer cake pans and bake 30 minutes at 350 degrees. (Ora always doubled the recipe for 3 big layers.) Cool and ice.

Icing: Cream 6 tablespoons soft butter with 1 egg yolk. Sift 3 cups powdered sugar, 1½ tablespoons cocoa, and 1 teaspoon cinnamon together. Add to creamed mixture alternating with hot, black coffee, beginning with 1½ tablespoons. Beat until smooth. If necessary, add a few more tablespoons coffee until icing spreads easily but thickly.

1½ cups sugar
¾ cup shortening
3 eggs, beaten
1¾ cups flour
½ teaspoon soda
½ teaspoon salt
¾ teaspoon nutmeg
1 teaspoon cinnamon
3 tablespoons cocoa
¾ cup sour buttermilk
1 teaspoon vanilla
1 teaspoon lemon extract
½ cup pecans, chopped and toasted

Kathleen's Chuck Wagon Cake

There was a day when almost every woman who baked had a recipe for a crumb-topped coffee cake. Kathleen Fritz, the 1924 bride of rancher Fred Fritz, had a chuck wagon version. Her supplies were packed on burros from Clifton. It took 118 crossings of the Blue River to get to the Fritz spread. Her basics included 600 pounds of flour, 400 pounds of sugar, coffee, salt, and canned milk, delivered twice a year to the XXX Ranch. That fueled the Fritzes for fencing 100 sections of land for their cows and horses.

Work flour, sugar, salt, and shortening in bowl to make fine crumbs. Remove ½ cup of crumbs for cake topping. To the remaining mixture, add baking powder, spices, and soda. Add the beaten eggs to the sour milk, which may be made by adding 1 tablespoon vinegar to 1 cup canned milk, if necessary. Add to dry mixture and beat until very smooth. Pour into well-greased biscuit pan (8 by 12 by 2 inches) and sprinkle crumbs on top. Bake at 400 degrees for 20 to 30 minutes. Serve from pan while hot. Nuts can be added to topping.

2½ cups flour
2 cups brown sugar
½ teaspoon salt
⅔ cup butter or lard
2 teaspoons baking powder
½ teaspoon cinnamon
½ teaspoon nutmeg
½ teaspoon soda
1 cup sour milk
2 eggs, well beaten

Bertha Palmer's Angel Food Cake

Mrs. E. Payne Palmer Sr. gathered her large family every Christmas Eve to sing carols, then feast on this Angel Food Cake, always inscribed, "Happy Birthday, Jesus." Bertha was an angel to Phoenix, helping bring famous musicians, then the Phoenix Symphony to town, as well as going door-to-door to raise funds to rebuild St. Joseph's Hospital when it burned. During the 1920s, she took her children, boxes of oranges, and a portable organ to St. Luke's Sanatorium to give tuberculosis patients a cheery concert. Bertha Palmer was named Arizona's first Mother of the Year.

whites of 8 or 9 eggs, 1 cup
¼ teaspoon salt
1 teaspoon cream of tartar
1 teaspoon vanilla or almond extract
1½ cups sugar
1 cup cake flour

Have egg whites at room temperature. Add salt and beat until frothy. Add cream of tartar and beat until very stiff but not dry. Add flavoring. Have ready flour and sugar, which have been sifted separately, then measured, then sifted together four times. Fold sugar and flour mixture gradually into beaten white mixture. Turn into ungreased angel food pan. Place cake in very slow oven, no higher than 250 degrees. Bake 50 minutes. Let rise slowly to top of pan. Increase heat gradually and let bake until set and well browned. Press finger at top of cake. If it springs back without leaving a dent, it is done. Invert to cool before removing.

Katie Raburn's Potato Chocolate Cake

Katie Raburn came to the Duncan area from Texas in the 1920s and made friends fast with her spicy, satiny, black walnut chocolate cake—the best possible use for a cup of left-over mashed potatoes. Her granddaughter, Dixie Jones, said this cake rated as high as tallow biscuits, a real old-timey treat to Katie.

1 cup fat (butter, lard)
2 cups sugar
½ cup milk
2 squares melted chocolate
1 cup mashed potatoes
4 eggs, well beaten
2 cups flour
4 teaspoons baking powder
3 teaspoons cinnamon
½ teaspoon nutmeg
¼ teaspoon cloves
1 cup black walnuts

Cream the fat, using butter, lard, shortening, whatever is on hand. Add the sugar, milk, chocolate, mashed potatoes, and eggs, beating well. Mix flour with baking powder and spices, then add to batter. Beat well, fold in nuts, and pour batter into a large (9 by 13-inch) pan that has been greased and floured. Bake 1 hour at 325 degrees. As cake cools, make Seven-Minute Icing.

Combine in a double boiler: 2 egg whites, 1½ cups sugar, ¼ teaspoon cream of tartar, and ⅔ cup of water. Place over boiling water and beat with rotary beater until mixture holds its shape and peaks. Fold in 1½ teaspoons vanilla. Beat until cool, then spread in snowy drifts over the cake. They just don't make cakes like this much anymore.

Kleiners and Black Walnut Cake

The Orme School on the 40,000-acre Quarter Circle V Bar Ranch in Yavapai County opened as an accommodation school in 1929. It became a nationally noted prep school under the leadership of Charles (Chic) Orme Sr., headmaster, rancher, and legislator. Ranch food supervision was managed capably by Minna Vrang Orme, whose specialties ranged from Kleiners (old Danish fried cookies) to the velvety crunch of Black Walnut Cake. The family boasted that Aunt Minna was "full Dane."

Kleiners

Take sugar and blend in eggs and butter and beat up well. Add now the rich milk, then beat in vanilla and brandy. Take flour and baking powder and sift into first mixture. Knead well, adding more flour if sticky. Roll thin, cut in 1 by 4-inch inch strips, slit in center, and turn one end through the slit. Cook in deep hot lard until golden brown.

Black Walnut Cake

Cream butter with sugar until smooth. Sift flour with salt and baking powder, then add alternately with milk. Fold in beaten egg whites and vanilla, then floured black walnuts. Bake 45 minutes at 350 degrees. Frost with Seven-Minute Icing, and top with scattering of black walnuts. Aunt Minna used Orme Ranch home-grown walnuts.

Kleiners

1 cup sugar
2 eggs
1 heaping tablespoon butter
½ cup rich milk
1 tablespoon vanilla extract
2 tablespoons brandy
3 cups flour or more
1 teaspoon baking powder

Black Walnut Cake

½ cup butter
⅓ cups sugar
3 cups sifted flour
pinch of salt
3 teaspoons baking powder
1 cup milk
4 egg whites, beaten
1 teaspoon vanilla
1 cup floured black walnuts

Holiday Cake Filling

Early American recipes are heavy with alcoholic beverages, which helped preserve fancy food in an era without refrigeration. Such a recipe was used during holidays by Sara J. Hay, mother of Margaret Thomas, longtime Arizona writer and former woman's page editor of The Arizona Republic. *Her filling preserved people as well as cake.*

Mix 3 egg whites, 6 egg yolks, and 1 cup of sugar with ½ cup of soft butter. Blend well. Add ½ cup rum and ½ cup sherry. Cook until thick. Add ½ cup nuts or any kind of fruit, whiskey soaked.

3 egg whites
6 egg yolks
1 cup sugar
½ cup soft butter
½ cup rum
½ cup sherry
½ cup nuts or fruit, whiskey soaked

Red Devil's Food Cake

One of the cake wonders of the good ol' days was Red Devil's Food—not really red, but a chocolate-red which sliced solidly with a moist crumb. Mrs. Ernie Davis made a blue-ribbon version, frosting it with chocolate sometimes, but for cake sales with Penuche Frosting as caramel brown as Panoche Creek, which ran on their ranch near Navajo Mountain. Panocha is a Mexican word for the solid cakes of brown sugar made by boiling down sugar cane.

Put butter into mixing bowl. Sift sugar, flour, soda, and salt together, then sift into bowl, blending with butter. Dissolve cocoa in boiling water and add to batter, mixing well. Add eggs, one at a time, then vanilla. Beat until glossy. Bake 25 to 30 minutes at 375 degrees in 2 greased, paper-lined layer cake pans.

½ cup soft butter
2 cups sugar
2½ cups sifted flour
1 heaping teaspoon soda
¼ teaspoon salt
⅔ cup best cocoa available
½ cup boiling water
2 eggs
1 teaspoon vanilla

Coconino County Penuche Frosting

Stir in heavy pan over a slow heat: 2 cups brown sugar, ¼ teaspoon salt, and 1 cup of cream or canned milk. Bring to a boil, then cook slowly, stirring, until frosting reaches the soft ball stage. Add a heaping tablespoon of butter. Remove from fire and let it cool a few minutes. Stir in 1 teaspoon vanilla and ½ cup nuts, then beat until thick and creamy. If too heavy, thin with a little cream. Make a double batch and pour the extra into a buttered pie plate for wonderful fudge.

Honey Cake

Every Jewish cook had her recipe for Honey Cake. One of the best came from Brenda Mechler, who was also a talented writer, successfully scriptwriting in Hollywood during the Garbo-Crawford years. She returned to Phoenix, which had become home in 1921 when the Mechlers bought alfalfa acreage near the Dwight B. Heard farms.

Sift together flour, baking powder, soda, and spices. Mix sugar, oil, and add eggs, one at a time. Stir into flour mixture alternately with honey, rinsing honey cup with hot coffee. Mix currants and nuts with tablespoon flour and citrus peel. Fold into batter. Turn into greased, brown-paper-lined, 9 by 13 by 2½-inch pan. Bake at 325 degrees for 1 hour, then at 300 degrees for 25 minutes. Invert pan and allow cake to cool before removing. Cut in diamond shapes or squares and strew with almonds.

4 cups sifted flour
2½ teaspoons baking powder
1 scant teaspoon soda
1 level teaspoon cinnamon
1 teaspoon grated nutmeg
2 cups sugar
1 tablespoon fine citrus peel
1 cup butter or oil
4 eggs, large
2 cups honey
1 cup strong coffee, hot
1 cup currants, chopped
1 cup chopped nuts
1 tablespoon flour

Eggless Sugarless Gingerbread

This eggless delight was baked on the long-gone X Slash Ranch in New Mexico, where Ethel Parker Harbison's father had moved three generations of his family. The ranch dried up and dried out before Arizona became a state, so the family came to Tucson and became great patrons of the University of Arizona. Ethel taught on the Navajo Reservation, especially enjoying their sings. On her salary, this gingerbread was just about the perfect dessert.

Mix molasses with soda and sour cream. Sift dry ingredients and combine with liquid ingredients. Add melted, cooled shortening and beat well. Bake in shallow 8 by 10-inch pan in 350-degree oven for 30 to 40 minutes until finger pressed lightly on middle leaves no indentation. "Do not overbake. The product is very velvety and delicious," Ethel said.

1 cup dark molasses
1 ¾ teaspoons soda
1 cup light sour cream
2 ½ cups flour
2 teaspoons ginger
1 teaspoon cinnamon
½ teaspoon cloves
¼ teaspoon salt
¼ cup shortening, melted and cooled

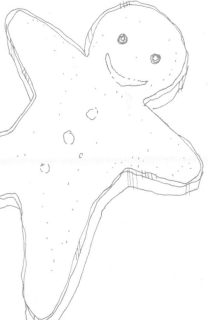

Wherever early residents made their homes, the kitchen was the center of the household. Mrs. Robert Kealy of Tucson set up housekeeping and cooked for her family in a converted boxcar.
ARIZONA HISTORICAL SOCIETY, TUCSON

Biscochitos (Sugar Cookies)

Pioneer women came to Arizona with hand-written recipes for treasured cookies dating back to the Mayflower, only to discover that a Mexican neighbor baked similar cookies—with names that were not at all the same. Perfect Sugar Cookies and Biscochitos, for instance, are both perfect sugar cookies.

1 pound sugar
1 pound flour
4 ounces cinnamon
1 pound butter or lard
1 dozen egg yolks
confectioner's sugar

Sift together sugar, flour, and cinnamon. Add to lard the egg yolks, then dry ingredients and mix well. With hands, fashion small balls of dough about the size of walnuts. Use a glass to flatten after placing balls on a greased cookie sheet, 1 inch apart. Bake 6 minutes in oven preheated to 325 degrees. While hot, sprinkle with confectioner's sugar.

Perfect Sugar Cookies (Mayflower era): Cream 1 cup butter and 1½ cups sugar, add 2 well beaten eggs, and blend. Dissolve ½ teaspoon soda in 3 tablespoons thick sour cream. Add with 3 cups flour and ¼ teaspoon salt to dough, then chill until very stiff. Roll thin as a coin on a floured board. Cut in Christmas shapes. Bake in a hot oven at 400 degrees until pale gold, not brown. Sprinkle lightly with pounded (granulated) sugar.

Scrolls (Trasce)

Wherever Hungarian and Slavic settlers in Arizona gathered for New Year's, in Bisbee or Globe-Miami or Phoenix, they crunched the golden goodness of Scrolls, delicately flavored with rum or brandy. Dimpled and merry Ann Bertchan had come here from near Belgrade the year Arizona became a state. At 75, she was still filling bowls with Scrolls, perfect with coffee, tea, or wine.

2 cups flour
1 tablespoon rum or brandy
½ teaspoon salt
12 egg yolks
1 cup oil or whipped shortening
½ cup sifted powdered sugar

Mix first four ingredients with hands until very smooth, about 15 minutes, until it leaves the sides of the bowl. Cut the amount in half and knead each half again. Roll paper-thin on floured board into long rectangles. Slice down and across into 3 by 5-inch pieces. Slash 2-inch slits, about ½ inch apart, in center of each. As cut, place in tea towel so dough will not dry out. Drop into hot oil or shortening in deep, heavy pan. Fry until golden, about one minute on each side. When gilded crisp, remove with fork by slits, allow to drain, then place in large bowl. As bowl fills, sprinkle with powdered sugar. Makes about 3 dozen and leaves 1 dozen egg whites for meringues or angel food cakes.

Grandmother Waterbury's Molasses Drops

Jack Humphrey was a geneticist who spent fourteen years in Switzerland perfecting use of seeing eye dogs. Then he and wife Nettie came to the Bard Ranch near Prescott, where he pioneered development of drought-resistant cattle. "In all those years, the one formula he could never put together was his grandmother's recipe for making the molasses cookies he hungered for," Nettie laughed. "Then his sister gave him the old recipe." Somewhere in most older men's pasts was a soft and chewy molasses cookie.

Cream butter and sugar; add molasses, then beaten egg. Dissolve soda in milk. Mix sifted flour, spices, and salt. Then alternately add liquid and dry mixtures to the creamed mixture. Sprinkle a bit of flour over raisins and add to batter. Drop by teaspoon on greased cookie sheet. Bake 12 to 15 minutes at 350 degrees.

½ cup butter
½ cup sugar
½ cup molasses
1 egg
1 teaspoon soda
½ cup sour milk
2 ½ cups sifted flour
1 ½ teaspoons cinnamon
¼ teaspoon cloves
½ teaspoon ginger
½ teaspoon salt
½ cup chopped raisins

100-Year-Old Oatmeal Cookies

In the chronology of cookies, sugar cookies came before oatmeal in popularity, then oatmeal advanced and passed molasses to tie with sugar varieties for all seasons—except Christmas. Billy Early, historian and early settler in Florence, contributed this recipe, in her family for generations.

Mix together the first four ingredients. Mix together the flour, oatmeal, soda, and cream of tartar. Combine both with vanilla until well blended. Add nuts or raisins, if desired. Roll in balls and place on cookie sheets. Bake for 10 minutes at 375 degrees. Makes 5 dozen.

½ cup butter, soft
2 eggs
1 cup white sugar
1 cup brown sugar
2 ½ cups white flour
1 cup oatmeal
¼ teaspoon soda
½ teaspoon cream of tartar
1 teaspoon vanilla
optional: 1 cup nuts and/or 1 cup raisins

Camelback Inn Anniversary Bars

Camelback Inn opened in 1936 and built its only-one-in-all-the-world reputation with care. For Manager Jack Stewart, an important part of growth was good, simple food, carefully seasoned to avoid harming the ulcer set. To his wife, care meant Camelback Inn Anniversary Bars. "Richer than Croesus," Louise Shoemaker Stewart used to say.

Cream butter with ½ cup brown sugar and the white sugar. Add 2 egg yolks, the flour, the water, vanilla, and a dash of salt. Mix well. Pat evenly on bottom of buttered and floured 8 by 16-inch baking dish. Sprinkle with the chocolate chips. Beat 4 egg whites until stiff enough to hold a peak. Slowly beat in the remaining brown sugar. When glossy and smooth, spread over chips. Bake 30 to 35 minutes in oven preset to 350 degrees. Cut in small squares; this yields 32 servings.

1 cup butter, soft
½ cup white sugar
2½ cups brown sugar
4 eggs, separated
2 cups flour
2 packages (12 ounce) chocolate chips
1 tablespoon water
1 tablespoon vanilla
dash of salt

Harvey House Chocolate Puffs

Fred Harvey, an Englishman with a genius for glamourizing travel and making it comfortable, solved the Santa Fe Railroad's food and lodging problems with his Spanish-themed hotel-restaurants. Arizona had five Harvey Houses along the main line—located in Winslow, Williams, Ash Fork, Seligman, and Kingman—as well as the venerable El Tovar and other facilities at the Grand Canyon. His Harvey Girls, ages 18 to 30, added a rare touch of feminine charm. Humorist Will Rogers once said, "Fred Harvey kept the West in food and wives."

Boil together flour, water, and butter. Remove from fire and beat in melted chocolate and eggs, one at a time. Bake in a gun pan (muffin tins), lightly greased, filled half full. Bake in hot oven (400 degrees) until done in peaks, 20 to 25 minutes.

Allow to cool, then cut off top of each cake and put in a teaspoon of strawberry preserves or fresh berries. Heap with sweetened whipped cream. I have no record of what happened to the tops, but I am positive they were not thrown out. Makes 10 Puffs.

1 cup flour
1 cup water
1½ cups butter
1 ounce chocolate, melted
3 eggs
1 teaspoon strawberry preserves or sugared fresh berries
whipped cream, sweetened

Ada Rigden's Sour Cream Doughnuts

Ada Eldred came to pleasant Kirkland Valley to teach school in 1905. She married cattle rancher Charles Rigden and helped bring women's club activities to the area. Well known as a talented artist, she also made doughnuts as pretty as a picture.

Mix all ingredients except flour. Add enough flour so that dough will not stick to a floured board, blending well. Roll and cut with a doughnut cutter. Fry in fresh deep fat.

1½ cups sugar
1½ cups sour milk
1½ cups thick sour cream
1 egg, beaten
2 level teaspoons soda
½ teaspoon salt
½ teaspoon nutmeg
2 cups flour or more

When a friend dropped in for a visit, Prescott-area rancher's wife Norah Clough entertained while keeping on with her kitchen chores, a custom that hasn't changed all that much since 1915. SHARLOT HALL MUSEUM

Empañadas de Dulce

"Nowhere in this country does the past walk with the present in greater rhythm than here. Here is history fading and history bursting into view—people of many cultures, mingling, learning from each other." So was written about Tucson's annual Festival of the Arts, presented each year following Easter. The Old Pueblo relived its ancestry from early-day Indian culture to Spanish, from pioneer to ranch heritage. Hundreds crammed the Placita to see and hear the mariachis (wandering minstrels), to break cascarones (confetti eggs), and to sit at street cafes and eat tacos, tamales, and sweet turnovers, Empañadas de Dulce.

2 cups flour
2 teaspoons baking powder
1 teaspoon salt
½ cup lard or butter
¼ cup water
fillings of applesauce, pineapple, peaches, mince meat, or pumpkin

Combine flour, baking powder, and salt. Blend in butter to crumbs. Add water and mix until pastry dough comes to a ball, leaving the side of the bowl. Roll out ⅛ inch thick. Cut 4-inch circles. (A can with both ends removed works well.) All fillings should be sweetened and spiced with cinnamon. Place a teaspoon of filling on half of each round. Moisten edges and fold dough in half over filling. Seal with fork or fingers at outer edge. Bake on cookie sheets 20 minutes at 375 degrees or deep fry in hot oil. Cool on racks or paper. Makes 15 to 20 turnovers—the Mexican cousin to Granny's fried pie.

Dried Apple Pies

I loathe, abhor, despise
    Abominate dried apple pies.
I like good bread,
    I like good meat,
Or anything that's fit to eat.
    But of all poor grub
    beneath the skies,
The poorest is dried apple pies.
    Give me the toothache or sore eyes
In preference to dried
      apple pies.

Contributed by a very positive Anonymous to The First Presbyterian Church of Florence *Centennial Recipe Book.*

Custard Pie

Roosevelt, originally the post office for the construction crew of the Theodore Roosevelt Dam, is now under waters impounded by the dam. Mrs. Ezra Peace of Roosevelt served many a piece of this silken custard pie before the village washed away.

Break eggs into a bowl and beat well. Mix flour in sugar and add mixture to eggs. Add milk and nutmeg and beat until sugar is dissolved. Pour into unbaked pie shell. Bake in moderate oven at 325 degrees an hour or until custard is set. Cool before slicing.

1 unbaked 10-inch pie shell
3 eggs
1½ tablespoons flour
1½ cups sugar
1½ cups milk
1 teaspoon nutmeg

Luscious Lemon Pie

Summer Sundays walking home from church as a young girl, I confess I thought with satisfaction of the clear, tart lemon and high, fresh coconut pies my mother always baked on Saturday. Which to have for dessert? When I grew up to write about food, plain lemon pie, or its pioneer substitute, vinegar pie, was almost every woman's specialty. This tangy version was given to me by Vermelle B. Cowley, then state Cowbelle president, of the Diamond L Ranch near St. Johns.

Mix flour, cornstarch, salt, and sugar together. Add lemon juice, then egg yolks. Then add boiling water and stir until smooth, cooking over high heat until thick. Pour into 9-inch baked pastry shell. Beat egg whites with 2 tablespoons sugar to make a meringue. Cover pie to the edges of crust and put in 300-degree oven until peaks are brown. Some people prefer their lemon pie topped with whipped cream.

1 cup sugar
5 tablespoons mixed flour and cornstarch
¼ teaspoon salt
5 tablespoons fresh lemon juice
2 egg yolks
2 cups boiling water

El's Peach Cobbler

"Stop where the trucks stop" became tourist advice in the early days of highways and trucking. On Route 89A west of Sedona, it was El's Place where cars and trucks were parked morning till night. Elma Zilliox and her mother, Lou, made traffic-halting pies and cobblers. When Sedona's peach crop came in, they couldn't bake enough of these.

Mix peaches, sugar, and 2 tablespoons flour and place in 8 by 10-inch pan. Dot with butter. Sprinkle with 2 teaspoons more sugar, cover with crust made by mixing water, shortening (half lard, half butter is best), flour, and salt. Bake on top shelf of oven at 450 degrees 20 minutes, or until browned.

1 quart fresh peaches, peeled and sliced
1 cup sugar
2 level tablespoons flour
¼ cup butter
2 teaspoons sugar
¼ cup water
½ cup shortening
1 cup flour
pinch of salt

Lula Mae's Hurry-Up Duff

Mrs. Jack Brooks began married life on a ranch on the Blue River in the White Mountains, with no water and no electricity, before REA. Cooking began with checking to see if the wood was chopped and by carrying water. "I never really learned to love cooking," she admitted with a twinkle. Collecting is her passion. Lula Mae has her own family museum—old-time cooking utensils as planters, framed bird points and trade beads, her grandsons' worn little chaps, stone tools, and stuffed animals. When it snowed or rained for days, the Brookses played anthropologist or taxidermist, self-taught.

Lula Mae learned to make all her kitchen minutes count. She gardens, cans, makes pickles and preserves, dries raisins, freezes berries, peaches, and vegetables. She is always ready for company and beginning with one quart of fruit, she can turn out her Hurry-Up dessert in half an hour. "Quick and easy as a box and it feeds more and better," she said.

¼ pound butter
1 cup sugar
1 cup, plus 2 tablespoons flour
1 cup milk
1 teaspoon baking powder
1 quart fruit with juice

Melt butter in 8 by 13-inch pan in moderate oven. Mix sugar, flour, milk, and baking powder and pour into melted butter. Stir lightly. Pour in 1 quart fruit and juice—apples, peaches, apricots, berries, or cherries. Distribute evenly, then bake at 325 degrees until crust forms and browns on top, about 30 minutes. Serve warm with table cream, ice cream, or whipped cream to 9—maybe 12, with enough cream.

John (Pie) Allen Apple Pie

John B. Allen is said to be the first man in Arizona to keep bees and sell honey. He became popular and well known thanks to his delectable apple pies, which he baked and sold daily from plank tables on the streets of Tucson. He was elected to the Territorial Legislature, using his nickname, "Pie," and successfully worked at moving the capital to Tucson from Prescott in 1867. After ten years, Prescott was again the capital. Who knows what would have happened if "Pie" had kept on baking his specialty, using freshly ground wheat, pure lard, fresh or dried apples, and honey-sugar?

pastry for 2-crust pie
5 or 6 tart apples, peeled, sliced thin
½ cup sugar, brown or white
¼ cup honey
1 teaspoon cinnamon
3 slices butter

Line deep, 9-inch pie plate with rolled pastry. Mix apples and sugar and cinnamon thoroughly. Mound in pie crust. Drizzle with honey and dot with butter. Cover with upper crust. Cut several slits in crust to allow steam to escape. Bake at 425 degrees 50 to 60 minutes until top crust is an appetizing light brown. Cool a bit before slicing.

Pastry: Work ⅔ cup of lard into 2 cups of flour, adding 1 teaspoon salt and 4 to 6 tablespoons cold water.

Boiled Puddings

The pioneer kitchen operated around an open hearth with many main dishes bubbling in the big cast iron kettle, often soups, mostly stews. Some inspired cook mixed a pudding and poured it into a floured bag and hooked it over the side to boil with the stew. Fruit dumplings, suet puddings, and egg batter puddings evolved. The camp cook added raisins (a "spotted pup" to the cowboy) and boiled his pudding in water. The wood range and such luxuries marked the end of boiled puddings except for the steamed plum pudding of holiday distinction.

1 cup molasses
1 cup water
salt
1 teaspoon soda
cornmeal or flour
spices

Molasses Pudding: Mix 1 cup molasses with a cup of water, a pinch of salt, and a teaspoon of soda. Add enough cornmeal or flour to make a thick batter and spice to taste. Pour into a floured pudding bag, tie at the top with a piece of cloth or string, and boil an hour or so. Serve hot with milk. Wash out bag for future use.

The Eggless Plum Pudding

Always a plum pudding but never a plum.

1 heaping cup bread crumbs, 2 cups flour, 1 cup suet, chopped fine, 1 cup raisins, 1 cup molasses, 1 cup sweet milk, 1 teaspoon soda, 1 teaspoon salt, 1 teaspoon cloves, 1 teaspoon cinnamon. Boil 2½ hours in a 2-quart pail.

From *The Frugal Housewife*, 1835

Lumpy Dick

The tiny, pine-nuzzled (elevation 5,813 feet) village of Strawberry in Gila County was named appropriately for the crimson dotted fields of wild strawberries once growing profusely in the area. Edith Peach Slaughter was born there in a log cabin in 1885. She grew up to teach school in Strawberry in another log cabin which had its 100th birthday in 1985. Edith did not make the party, but one of her legacies is a pudding with a most descriptive name: Lumpy Dick.

2 cups flour
water
1 teaspoon salt
1 quart milk
¼ pound butter

Mix flour and salt. Add just enough water to form into lumps. Heat milk to scalding point, being careful not to burn. Stir the lumpy flour into the hot milk and heat with the butter, but do not mix well.

"This was served in the evening outside in the yard to the children and, oh, what a treat they thought it was, with brown sugar or strawberry jam as a little topping," Edith told a group of children who belonged to the Slurpee and frozen yogurt age. Recipe serves 4 to 5 children.

Kolb Corn Pudding

Emory C. Kolb's first look at the awesome Grand Canyon of the Colorado was in 1902. The instant love affair never ended. He and his brother, Ellsworth, made the Canyon their life work, guiding the famous through, making photographic history, packing the house at Carnegie Music Hall. Emory never weighed more than 115 pounds. He could run the mule trail to the South Rim and beat the mules by almost an hour. One of his favorite nutritious dishes was Corn Pudding as prepared by Inez Tewawina, a Hopi girl the Kolbs made part of the family. Try it: Kolb lived to be 90, never moving from his beloved home on the Canyon rim.

2½ cups milk
3 tablespoons fresh cornmeal
½ cup molasses or brown sugar
2 tablespoons butter
2 eggs
pinch of salt
ground cinnamon and ginger, optional

Set oven to 300 degrees. Heat milk in large pan until scalded; do not boil. Add cornmeal, one spoon at a time, stirring well after each addition. Add molasses and butter. Reduce heat to low and cook 10 to 15 minutes. Stir often until it thickens. In a medium bowl, beat eggs with a whisk. Add salt, cinnamon, and ginger. Slowly add the cornmeal mixture to the egg mixture, beating constantly. Butter a deep oven dish. Bake for 45 minutes. Serve Corn Pudding, also known as Indian Pudding, warm with cream or ice cream—not traditional but good.

Capirotada
(Bread Pudding)

Bread pudding traditionally has been the way to use old bread, and nobody does it better than Pueblo and Mexican cooks. Cheese and brown sugar, raisins and peanuts, and a cinnamon syrup over all blend in a pudding that warms and spices. The ranch and camp cook often took bread crumbs to make a raisin-studded suet pudding. This recipe is from Iris Jackson's collection of Heard Museum heritage fiesta foods.

Fry or toast bread cubes in butter until light brown, stirring often. As they toast, crush panocha and combine with the water. Boil until sugar dissolves, stirring. Add raisins and spices and simmer to a medium syrup. Meanwhile, place half the toasted bread in a solid layer and top with a thin layer of cheese, using a deep baking dish. Over that, sprinkle peanuts, pecans, and some raisins from the syrup. Top with a little syrup, evenly poured. Repeat layers until all ingredients are used. Bake in a 350-degree oven until firm and well done, 30 to 40 minutes. Serve warm.

½ cup butter
2 cups panocha or brown sugar
4 cups bread cubes
½ cup water
1 cup raisins
1 cup mixed peanuts and pecans
½ pound cheese, sliced
1 teaspoon cinnamon
½ teaspoon anise seed
½ teaspoon cloves

Anne's Date Pudding

Ann Rhodes (Mrs. Evertt P.) Johnson, retired Maricopa County schoolteacher, won awards for her children's short stories and a date-filled book for young students of Arizona history. Her own family is notable for its public service. Her brother, John J. Rhodes, became minority leader of the U.S. House of Representatives. But he couldn't match her Date Pudding.

Sift sugar, flour, salt, and baking powder together. Add dates, nuts, and milk. Blend well and pour into deep oiled pan. Mix hot water, brown sugar, and butter and heat in saucepan until sugar and butter melt together. Pour over batter. Bake in slow oven at 275 degrees for an hour. Serve hot or cold with whipped cream—a meltingly tender, slightly chewy, dessert deluxe.

1 cup white sugar
1 cup flour
⅛ teaspoon salt
2 teaspoons baking powder
1 cup dates, cut fine
½ cup dates
½ cup milk
2 cups hot water
1 cup brown sugar
1 tablespoon butter
whipped cream

Canned Date Pudding

"There's almost any vegetable or fruit you can name on the shelves and I can tomato juice, sauce, and catsup, soups and chili, my own kraut, and corn by the crate. I expect I save at least fifty dollars a month by canning. I watch at the produce places and when beans are eight cents a pound and peaches are cheap by the crate, we buy. I couldn't make it without Cecil. He's been disabled for years but he snaps beans, tightens lids, helps chop and, most important, he stands back and admires what I do."

Velma and J. C. Goldston brought Oklahoma values and customs and old family oil lamps and butter churns and iron kettles to Phoenix in the '30s along with recipes to can everything from beef tongue to date pudding. Their floor-to-ceiling shelves of glass-trapped fruits and vegetables reflected the almost-lost art of canning and preserving enough supplies every summer to last all year with plenty for any friend or relative who dropped in. Even then, few could can a pudding like Velma could, using Arizona eggs, raisins, dates, pecans, and apples.

3 eggs
1 cup brown sugar, packed
1½ teaspoons salt
1 teaspoon cinnamon
¼ teaspoon each, cloves and allspice
1½ cups fine, dry bread crumbs
1 cup each currants, raisins, chopped dates
1 cup finely chopped tart apples
4 ounces candied citron
1 cup broken pecans
1 cup water
½ cup chopped suet

Beat eggs well. Add sugar, salt, and spices. Mix bread crumbs and flour with nuts, fruit, and suet and add alternately with water to egg mixture. Stir well. Pack into greased pint jars to within 2 inches of top. Adjust caps. Process 2 hours at 5 pounds pressure. Yields 4 pints. Remove cap or loosen top to let steam escape and set pudding in pan of hot water before serving—pudding fit for the Cratchit family and Scrooge.

Buttermilk Fudge

Essie Bradshaw's Phoenix kitchen was hanging with well-used wooden corn and cabbage cutters, spoons, and butter paddles. Her holiday specialty was Buttermilk Fudge, made by her grandmother's recipe, older than churns, she said. "Try to get real buttermilk with little specks of butter," she advised.

1 cup buttermilk
1 teaspoon soda
2 cups white sugar
butter the size of a walnut
1 cup broken nutmeats

Pour buttermilk into heavy-bottom saucepan. Stir in soda to dissolve, then sugar, and cook, stirring constantly. It scorches easily so watch heat. Add butter and keep stirring. Remove a little to drop into a cup of water. If it forms a soft ball, remove from heat. When cool, beat until it thickens to fudge. Add walnuts, pecans, or hickory nuts and spread into buttered pie plate. Score into squares and eat all the round pieces as soon as fudge sets up (firms).

Divinity Candy

Carlotta and Don Pace, who lived over sixty-five years of their wedded life in Graham County, bought the historic Apache Indian Agency at Old San Carlos for $506 just before it was to be flooded by the newly built Coolidge Dam. He salvaged the buildings, pipe, and stone and sold it all. The Paces helped establish the Red Cross, PTA, Crippled Children's Association, and, later, Civil Defense, in Thatcher. Carlotta was never so busy, though, that she neglected Mormon Church duties, where she brought a touch of food heaven with her angel food cake and earthly Divinity.

3 cups sugar
1 cup corn syrup
1 cup water
3 egg whites, beaten stiff
1 cup nuts, chopped
1 teaspoon vanilla

Combine sugar, corn syrup, and water, then boil to the soft ball stage. Pour half boiled mixture over beaten egg whites and continue beating while the remainder boils until it spins a brittle thread off a spoon. Then add to egg mixture, continuing to beat while adding nuts and vanilla. This candy may be poured into a buttered flat dish or dropped on waxed paper from a teaspoon. Divinity Candy takes determination, but when it melts in your mouth, the memory of all that beating is gone. It was known as the daintiest of candies.

(LEFT) Like all the rooms at the Hubbell Trading Post, this dining area of the main hall provided vivid display space for Indian arts and crafts which Don Lorenzo Hubbell did so much to encourage, develop, and promote. NATIONAL PARK SERVICE

Aunt Bessie's Candy

Claire Champie Cordes and her six sisters and three brothers grew up on the Champie ranch, four miles from Castle Hot Springs. When times were hard, Claire put on the candy kettle. It seemed everybody wanted Claire's candies. "I'd make it and get on my horse and deliver it. Or take it to the store at Mayer and they'd sell it. They just went batty over Bessie's candy." Still do. In her eighties, Claire made this to bribe a nephew to take her fishing.

6 cups sugar
2 cups white Karo syrup
1 can (14-ounce) evaporated milk
½ pound butter
1 ¼ teaspoons salt
2 cups nuts

Blend sugar, Karo, milk, and salt with butter, which should be set out early to soften. Bring mixture to a rolling boil in a heavy saucepan. Add nuts. "Cooking the nuts is the secret. And butter. Don't use margarine. It isn't even real," Claire said. Cook candy to a firm ball when a half-spoonful is dropped into cold water or hold at 240 degrees on a candy thermometer. Keep stirring until candy reaches firm ball stage. Remove from heat and allow to cool, then beat until it starts to firm up. Spread on oiled pan or drop by spoon. Claire pours and cuts. Makes 2 pounds of old-fashioned goodness.

Jessie and Floyd Lamberson

Jessie and Floyd Lamberson retired in Phoenix after fifty years of life on assorted ranches, where every spring they filled in the mouse holes so rattlers couldn't get in. "Jessie made a hand you couldn't beat. She rode, kept the weights and the books, was right there for dippin' or brandin'—but she makes pies just a little bit better than anything else," Floyd said.

Grandmother's buttermilk pie, Grandma Moore's cream pie, green tomato pie, and Aunt Mag's chocolate pie—Jessie made all of them. "But I have a few sad cake stories." she said.

"When we were young and on the ranch, I beat up seventy-five egg whites to make a special angel food cake for my father's birthday. Eggs didn't mean a thing on the ranch. I baked it in a dishpan and it got so high. We put a glass with a rose in the center and carried it on a bread board by wagon into town. After he ate a piece, Daddy said, 'I'd much rather have one of your punkin pies.' And when our son Billy comes, he wants two cherry pies, two buttermilk pies, and two of grandma's cream pies with a batch of doughnuts, and he starts on that for breakfast."

And nary a cake.

Wood Stove Popcorn

The lumbering town of McNary began as Cluff Cienega (meadow), named by the Cluff brothers, who cut wild hay there for the livestock at Fort Apache. By 1924 it was a saw-mill town, and the name was changed by J.G. McNary. Every-one used wood stoves, and on hers, Alma Gray made popcorn into caramel pleasure for me with her old-time recipe, ready to eat in less than fifteen minutes.

Put 3 tablespoons popcorn into Dutch oven over good hot fire in wood stove. Cover and let it pop, uncovering to remove about a quart, then shaking the rest over the heat. Melt butter in a big roaster pan. Stir in the sugar and syrup with a wooden spoon. Bring it to a good boil on top of stove. Remove from heat; stir in vanilla, then baking soda, which will make syrup foam. Add popped corn to caramel syrup and stir to coat kernels. Put pan in slow oven and allow to bake about 8 minutes. Grease hands well if you want to make pop-corn balls, and place them on buttered platter. Otherwise, stir and eat as soon as it cools to mouth temperature.

3 quarts popped corn
1 stick (½ cup) butter
1 cup brown sugar
¼ cup corn syrup
1 teaspoon vanilla extract
¼ teaspoon baking soda

Dessert in the '20s.

"We had all kinds of desserts. Blanc mange, boiled custard, invariably served in plain glass cups with whipped cream on top, homemade ice-cream, fruit gelatin out of the box with that innocent-eyed little calf's head on it—but best was cobblers.

"There was a kind of calendar of cobblers. First came the dewberries, then the blackberries; than a triumphant pause for strawberry shortcake. Then came the peach cobblers.

"You could smell a peach cobbler all through dinner. I don't doubt if Esau had exchanged his birthright for a fresh peach cobbler he would never have regretted it. Cobblers came to the table in the longest of black pans and were put in front of Mama. The top of the pan was covered with rich pastry rolled thicker than for pie and it was laid over layers and layers of sliced peaches (fifty cents a bushel) with lots of sugar and a little flour and cinnamon and chunks—not dabs—of but-ter. The juice bubbled and oozed through the gashes cut like fern fronds in the brown crust. That juice was pinkish with a faint hint of mauve and it had an irri-descent overlay of tiny yellow spots of melted butter. Mama served it in cut glass berry dishes and we poured the bowls full of cream. I loved to watch the cream curdle ever so little around the edges. That was one dish where the last bite was as good as the first.

"Fruit cake was for Christmas and so were mince pies. Ambrosia was always served at Christmas, a dish that deserves its fancy name. Oranges and pineapple cut up, sweetened, and smothered in fresh grated coconut. It was served from the big glass punch bowl into clear glass cups. Just regular fare. Goodness knows we didn't have money."

Alberta Wilson Conant, *The Southwest Review*

Ice Cream

In March 1923, when Mrs. Simon Kander produced the twelfth edition of the fat, gray *Settlement Cook Book, The Way to a Man's Heart*, the all-encompassing art of preparing food at home was at its peak. The accomplished cook gardened, gathered, dried, canned, preserved, baked, fried, roasted, boiled, boned, crumbed, skinned, ground, or chopped anything and everything the family ate. Sunday dinner often began with an axe—to kill the chicken and to crush the ice.

Everybody's favorite frozen dessert began with this general rule: "Place ice in a burlap bag and pound with the broad side of an axe or hatchet to crush easily. The ice must be finely crushed."

Vanilla ice cream was made one of four ways: with cream, with whole eggs and cream (New York style), with gelatin, or with cornstarch and hot milk—but every recipe contained one quart cream. Other flavors ranged from Chocolate Coffee to Chestnut to Prune! For the adventurous, there were recipes for ices, sherbets, frappés, bombes, mousses, frozen puddings, and parfaits.

Countless times when I talked with pioneers about oldtime cooking, they mentioned "licking the ice cream dasher" as a favorite memory.

Not one mentioned the axe.

Custard Vanilla Ice Cream

The Richard Hartzler family drove a 1919 Model T Ford touring car with a brand on the wood. "It came out of Ajo and we had to drive it to Mexico. To get it across the border and back, it had to be branded like cattle," Polly Hartzler explained. No explanation needed for the all-time favorite ice cream they served every Fourth of July, the birthday of not just this country but of Polly and her father.

Allow 4 or 5 measures of cracked ice to 1 measure rock salt. More salt makes the cream freeze faster. Pack freezer ⅓ full of ice. Then alternate layers of salt and ice. Heat milk, sugar, salt, and slightly beaten eggs in top of double boiler over water until mixture reaches the boiling point. Stir constantly until custard coats the spoon. Remove from heat and cool. Add cream and vanilla. Fill freezer container and crank away.

2½ cups milk
1 cup sugar
⅛ teaspoon salt
2 eggs
1 quart light cream
2 teaspoons vanilla

Heritage Ice Cream

Scoop out vanilla ice cream in balls, with patent spoon, dip in fresh grated coconut or chopped nuts, arrange on platter with fern leaves. Pass the hot sauces.

Hot Fudge Sauce

Boil sugar and water 2 minutes. Add salt and arrowroot (or cornstarch) dissolved in a little cold water. Boil and stir until smooth and clear. Melt chocolate. Add to syrup, cook 3 minutes, add vanilla. Pour hot over vanilla ice cream. (My grandmother added 1 tablespoon butter.)

Butterscotch Sauce

Mix sugar and cornstarch. Place all together in saucepan and boil until a soft ball will form in cold water. Serve hot.

Maple Sauce

Boil 1 pint maple syrup and ¼ cup butter until it forms a thread when dropped from spoon. Serve hot.

From *The Settlement Cook Book*, 1921

Hot Fudge
1½ cups water
1 cup sugar
2 squares chocolate
1 tablespoon arrowroot
pinch salt
1 teaspoon vanilla

Butterscotch
4 tablespoons butter
1 cup brown sugar
1 teaspoon cornstarch
½ tablespoon vinegar
¼ cup water

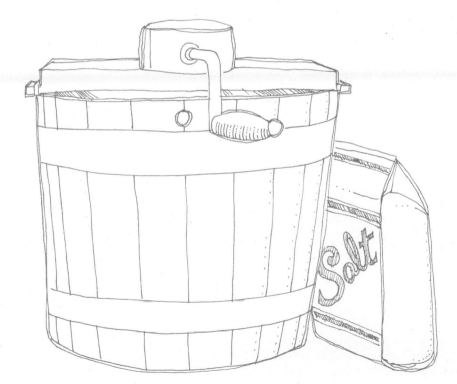

Chapter 11
Putting It Up and Putting It Down

From the beginning, women sought to preserve food at its peak for a later date. They either put it up—in baskets, pots and jars—or put it down—in the ground, in the cellar, or layered with care, mostly in crocks.

Pickling goes back to folk medicine. Cleopatra persuaded Caesar that pickles were a health food. Captain Cook took sauerkraut to sea to prevent scurvy.

Coming from Pennsylvania seven-sweet-and-seven-sour territory, I grew up with canning and pickling and jamming. Some of our family recipes went back before Civil War days. What a delight to discover some of those in the old handwritten receipt books of many families who came West.

Prickly Pear Preserves and Pyracantha Berry Jelly were not among those. Arizona's sweets and sours are distinctively its own, adding a tiny, hot, yellow pepper here and a cactus pad there.

Preservation and cooling prior to the ice box was ingenious. Dorothy Hubbell, daughter-in-law of Indian Trader Lorenzo Hubbell, described the non-powered cooler made for storage of milk, butter, and other supplies. It was a cabinet of three large, rimmed, tin shelves covered with strips of heavy material which were wet down, then kept damp. Meat was in a cool, dry place, usually well-salted. Don Lorenzo's home, now a part of the Hubbell Trading Post National Historic Site, was used like a baronial castle, where he entertained the famous.

The preservation of food without a good springhouse or ice was no problem for the wise. Stella Hughes, food historian, wrote about Clair Haight, who taught her a thing or two: "He was adept at putting down food for long keeping. Here at his own little home-stead south of Winslow, he kept eggs in waterglass for as long as a year. Here were crocks of homemade butter that kept fresh and sweet for months. There were shelves groaning with homemade cheese—and cabbage, wrapped in newspaper, that kept all winter. Pumpkins and winter squash stored likewise.

"He made jerky from beef and elk and venison, hanging from rafters in sacks. He put up his own sausage by frying patties and layering them in crocks and pouring the melted lard over them. No woman could beat his snow-white, tender hominy."

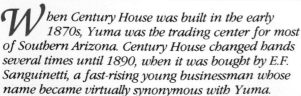

*W*hen Century House was built in the early 1870s, Yuma was the trading center for most of Southern Arizona. Century House changed hands several times until 1890, when it was bought by E.F. Sanguinetti, a fast-rising young businessman whose name became virtually synonymous with Yuma.

As a fifteen-year-old, Sanguinetti ignored advice from all sides when he forsook Southern California for Yuma. When the town flowered, with the young merchant as a recognized leader, so did the estate he was developing around Century House. One of his greatest delights was showing his gardens and aviary to guests. This colorful picture of canned foods was taken against a rainy window pane, a rare situation in Yuma.

Today, the oasis Sanguinetti developed at Century House still is enjoyed by visitors. Since 1965, it has been open to the public, and it now is operated by the Arizona Historical Society.

Prickly Pear Jelly

Cautiously admiring the prickly curves of the Opuntia, or prickly pear cactus, it is difficult to believe hundreds of recipes have been concocted from its stems (also called pads or leaves) and its tuna (fruit). Stewed, pickled, shredded, baked, candied, and crushed, the nopales (young pads) and fruit fed the ancient ones as well as desert newcomers. Mrs. Carlos Elmer and her gifted photographer husband of Kingman are Arizona specialists. Wilma makes the jelly recipe sound almost easy.

4 cups prickly pear juice
1 box powdered pectin (2-ounce box)
5 cups sugar

Line pail with plastic bag, use kitchen tongs and gloves and pick 40 to 50 ripe fruit from cactus. Not overripe; they squash. Carefully clean off stickers with a vegetable brush or singe off over a flame, holding fruit with a long-handled fork. Wash under running water and cut in half. Place in kettle over low heat. Add water to cover; if fruit are ripe and juicy, you may need no more than a half-cup. Boil 15 to 20 minutes. Press through 2 layers of cheesecloth into bowl, using wooden paddle or masher. Allow time for sediment to settle or let juice drip through a jelly bag. Combine 4 cups of juice with pectin and 5 cups of sugar. Boil hard 5 minutes. Skim foam off and pour into 7 sterilized jelly glasses. The color is a lovely, green-tinged red. The flavor is superb.

Wilcox Gold

Mrs. Jay Wilcox lived in a circle of citrus the family planted when the Milky Way Ranch was 'way out on Camelback Road in Phoenix. She turned the sunny fruit into jam and candy.

Scotch Orange Marmalade

2 large sweet oranges, about 1 pound
2 large lemons, about ½ pound
1 plump grapefruit
water
sugar

Cut washed fruit into eighths, then into fine slivers. Remove seeds and put them into half-cup of water. Weigh the cut fruit and add 6 cups water for each pound. Let seeds and fruit stand overnight in water. Next day, strain water from seeds into fruit. Simmer over low heat 1½ hours. Remove from heat to cool. Measure cooked fruit. Add 2½ cups sugar for each 2 cups (pint) of fruit. Stir in sugar. Stir over low heat until dissolved, then bring to a rapid boil. Cook 10 minutes or more until marmalade will set to clear jell. Cool, stir again, and seal in hot, sterilized jam jars.

Old-Fashioned Candied Citrus Peel

4 cups citrus peel, in strips
water to cover
4 cups sugar
1 cup water

Select thick-skinned fruit. Cut off peel and soak in cold water overnight. Cut peel into strips, cover with cold water and boil. Drain. Repeat 3 times. Measure 4 cups, then place in heavy pan with 4 cups sugar and 1 cup water. Simmer until all syrup is absorbed into peel. Place on racks to dry, then roll in sugar. Store in tins. A popular and inexpensive snack.

Mule Mountain Mince Meat

Amy Rose brought this 1880 recipe to Mule Mountain territory in Cochise County. Originally venison was used with kidney suet, but beef and its suet made their way into what has become a winter holiday pie of distinction.

Cook the meat and suet together until tender. Put through food grinder, coarse. Core and peel apples and grind coarse. Combine all ingredients in large kettle until apples and citron are tender and kitchen smells like spice heaven. Makes about 14 quarts, which may be augmented with brandy or bourbon, according to the tastes of those to be served. Mince meat is baked in a two-crust pie or in mince tarts served with brandy sauce.

Mule Mountain Memories, Bisbee Cook Book

4 pounds beef or game
1½ pounds suet
12 pounds apples, ground coarse
4 pounds raisins
2 pounds currants
½ pound citron
7 pounds sugar
2½ quarts cider
1 quart beef broth
16 teaspoons cinnamon, or less to taste
5 teaspoons ground cloves
2 teaspoons black pepper
5 teaspoons nutmeg

Watermelon Pickles

At an Arizona State Fair pickling demonstration, I learned the secrets of crisp, clear, jade-green watermelon pickles. The rind is better if the melon is not too ripe. The pink part of the melon will not crisp up. A pound of rind equals a quart of rind, which makes a pint of pickles. You can cut about five pounds of rind from a fifteen-pound watermelon.

Cut the green outer rind from the melon, leaving the white. Chunk in bite-size pieces. Put in canning kettle with 3 quarts water and ⅓ cup of salt (some old-time cooks used 2 teaspoons of alum). Bring to a boil and boil an hour or until firm. Rinse 4 times in clear water. Have ready pickle syrup, ingredients on right.

Bring syrup to a boil, then add rind. Simmer 1 hour; set aside. Second day, put rind into hot, sterile jars. To the syrup, add another cup of sugar and bring to a boil. Pour over rind in jars. Seal. Put into oven at 250 degrees for 20 minutes. Remove, cool, and hide until Thanksgiving.

5½ cups sugar
1 tablespoon whole cloves
1 cup water
2 sticks cinnamon
2 cups vinegar
sliced lemon

Pickled First Crop Figs

Juanita Harelson of Tempe learned to cook after marrying Jim, but when their four boys were small she had more fun teaching them sports—as a former Morenci physical education teacher. As the boys' appetites grew, Juanita discovered she loved cooking, entertaining, and canning. Pickled First Crop Figs kept that seedy fruit available year around.

Make syrup of: 1 cup water, 1 cup vinegar, 6 cups sugar, and 2 tablespoons mixed pickling spices tied in cheesecloth. Blanch 5 to 7 pounds of ripe figs in boiling water. Drain and boil in syrup for 10 minutes on 3 consecutive mornings. Do not remove from pan. Juanita used a large roaster, just pushing it to the back of the stove each day after boiling. Pack into hot, sterilized jars the third day. Cap tightly and store. Makes 4 quarts.

1 cup water
1 cup vinegar
6 cups sugar
2 tablespoons mixed pickling spices
5 to 7 pounds ripe figs

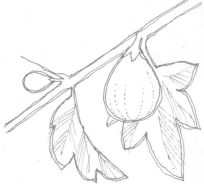

Strawberry Preserves

Vi and Harry Irving owned the post office and general store in Skull Valley for many years, in an era when operating a store was akin to printing the local newspaper. News and recipes were traded daily. Vi wound up knowing the best way to cook almost anything, or two ways to do the same thing.

3 quarts clean strawberries
5 cups sugar
2 cups berry juice

Weigh out 2 pounds washed, stemmed berries. Stir together the sugar and the berry juice (or water, but juice makes better, more colorful preserves). Add berries, cover, and bring to a boil. Remove the cover and boil rapidly 15 minutes. Cooking rapidly helps retain bright color and best flavor. Slide off heat and re-cover. Allow to stand and jell up overnight—this in an era when there was no powdered pectin. Pour into hot, sterilized jelly glasses and cover with paraffin.

Sunshine Strawberries: Measure equal weights of fruit and sugar. Layer into the preserving kettle the strawberries, then the sugar, in layers, each layer no more than 2 inches deep. Heat to boiling and skim off foam. Then boil rapidly 10 minutes. Pour berries onto platter in a single layer. Cover with plain window glass and let stand in the hot sun a full day. Put into jam jars and cover with paraffin before sealing. Very tasty.

Every Arizona county boasted of its farm and ranch production, and put together exhibits to prove its point. Navajo County sent these samples of potatoes, corn, and other produce to the Yavapai County Fair in the 1930s. SHARLOT HALL MUSEUM

Pickled Peaches

For decades, any vacant spot on the plate was filled with something pickled, often a clove-studded Pickled Peach. Walter Jordan, born in Verde Valley, was a pioneer fruit grower in Sedona. His Elberta and Hal-berta peaches were prized all over the state and shipped from California to Minnesota, chin-sticky juicy for pie, cobbler, and pickling.

Mix all ingredients except peaches in large kettle. Drop in peaches, a cup at a time. Bring to a boil, then reduce to a simmer until peaches are tender. Pack in sterilized jars and cover with cooking liquid. Seal.

10 pounds ripe peaches, peeled
5 pounds sugar
1 cup water
1 cup cider vinegar
1 teaspoon soda
1 teaspoon cinnamon
1 teaspoon nutmeg
2 tablespoons whole cloves

Ladies Aid Tomato Catsup

Nothing in a commercially prepared bottle packed the spicy spunk of Mrs. Tom Drum's homemade catsup.

Cook ½ gallon tomatoes until tender. Rub through a colander, add 1 heaping teaspoon each of allspice, cloves, nutmeg, mace, cinnamon, mustard, red pepper, and ginger. Set on slow fire and simmer for 3 hours. Bottle while warm and seal.

Flagstaff Cook Book, 1896
Ladies Aid of the Methodist Episcopal Church

½ gallon tomatoes

1 heaping teaspoon each of allspice, cloves, nutmeg, mace, cinnamon, mustard, red pepper, and ginger

Mustard Beans

Cook 1 peck string beans in salt water until done, then drain. For dressing: mix 3 pints of vinegar, 2 glasses of mustard, and 3 cups of brown sugar. When boiling, add 4 tablespoons of flour for thickening. then add beans, 5 onions, 5 mangoes (sweet bell peppers, 3 red and 2 green), 1 spoonful black pepper and boil 5 minutes. This makes 4 quarts.

Dried Tomatoes

Take ripe tomatoes, scald them with boiling water and strip off the skins or mash and squeeze them through a sieve. Stew the pulp slowly so to evaporate as much juice as possible without burning. Spread on plates and dry in slow oven or hot sun. When wanted for use, you have only to soak and cool a few minutes, then serve tomatoes like fresh from the garden.
From Lorraine Burke's *Cooking in the West,* all recipes 100 years old or older.

Paddock Pickles

Fred Paddock was Mayor of Phoenix twice, but his real claim to fame was the Lily Ice Cream Company, which he founded in 1920. There are many old jokes about ice cream and pickles, but Blanche Paddock's Cucumber Pickles were no joke. Ready to eat in two days, these pickles could be kept on the shelf indefinitely.

Pour vinegar into big crock. Mix dry ingredients, then add to vinegar and stir until dissolved. Pack clean, dry pickles into jars. Pour vinegar mixture over them. Seal. Shake occasionally. Smallest pickles will be ready to eat in 2 days. Fresh pickles may be added to jar as first pickles are used. These delicious sour pickles are a little more crisp if refrigerated, but it is not necessary to do so.

cucumbers, any size, fresh picked
1 gallon vinegar
1 cup dry mustard
1 cup sugar
1 cup salt

Uncooked Sweet Relish

Tasty with meat or beans, this relish recipe was given to me by everyone from Mormon pioneers to third-generation Arizona farm wives to University of Arizona Extension Service teachers.

Wash all vegetables and remove spots and seeds. Chop fine, mix with remaining ingredients, and let stand overnight. In morning, pack into sterilized jars and seal at once. Don't bother to can if you'll refrigerate and use soon or give away. Makes 5 or 6 pint jars.

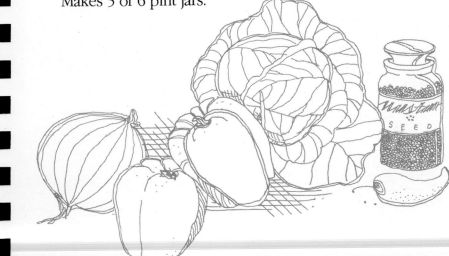

1 quart cabbage, chopped fine
1 pint white onions, chopped fine
1 pint sweet red peppers, chopped fine
1 pint sweet green peppers, chopped fine
4 tablespoons mustard seed
1 quart vinegar
4 cups sugar
2 teaspoons celery seed
2 or 3 hot peppers, chopped fine
5 tablespoons salt

Chapter 12
Wild in the Pan

Heritage food in Arizona began free with nature's bounty, always used by the Indians and often tried by the pioneer.

Rather ironically, it is now being gathered more and more by the increasingly sophisticated desert and forest visitor.

The instinctive cook never is satisfied to use anything as it is. If raw, it must be chopped, grated, cooked, or sauced. If sour, add something sweet. If sweet, add something tart. If it is almost inedible, grind it. It's the ancestral way.

The free Indian market was a delicatessen of variety and substance—in a wild state. Beans, fruits, seeds, plants, greens, roots, honey, squash, and melons were there for the cost of labor. Most gathering was done with family or friends, a sociable time—the aboriginal version of a business lunch.

The hunters, men and boys , provided the meat, from small game and birds to deer, antelope, bear, and an occasional bighorn sheep. Fish were plentiful, but forbidden eating for some tribes because of ancestral legends.

As settlers from all ethnic groups cleared land, they, too, used God's bounty. The vegetables were usually flavored with meat drippings or butter, and fruits sometimes were sweetened with sugar from the maple or the bee. The mustard seed went into table mustard; the elderberry into cobbler; the wild grape into jelly.

The kitchen challenge of the edible wild was extended later by more sophisticated cooks who dressed the wild mushroom in crumbs and wine and the greens with vinegar and bacon. Some preferred to make a marmalade with cactus or to use the brilliant red of saguaro fruit to make an exotic sundae—new heritage, free-food cooking to pass on to another generation.

Approaching from the right direction, it is easy to see the Gila Indian Center as a giant snake, coiled in the desert setting of the Gila River Indian Reservation, rattlers extended upward. The architects may have been inspired by its proximity to Snaketown, a prehistoric Hohokam Indian Village located nearby.

The center itself spans the centuries from the culture of the Hohokam, who disappeared in the fifteenth century, to the most recent hundred years of the Pimas and Maricopas who inhabit the area. It also provides an impressive showcase for the original art and craftwork of some thirty Indian tribes of the American Southwest and Northern Mexico.

One of the leading Indian-owned cultural centers

in the nation, it attracts well over a quarter-million visitors annually.

A tribal corporation owned by the Gila River Indian Community opened the center in 1971, on a site thirty miles south of Phoenix at the junction of Interstate 10 and Arizona Route 93. With its arts and crafts shop, museum, restaurant, and outdoor Gila Heritage Park, it gives Phoenix-area visitors their easiest and nearest opportunity to visit an Indian reservation and see the traditional lifestyle, beautiful artwork, and original crafts of Native Americans.

The Gila Indian Center is open from 8 A.M. to 6 P.M., seven days a week, except for major holidays.

Mesquite Beans

The most dependable food the old-time desert Indians had was from the mesquite tree. The gold or red-streaked bean it produced, sometimes twice a year, was more important to Arizona desert dwellers than corn or wheat. Historian Roscoe Willson called it "the means of the desert, " and Kearney and Peebles in their scholarly books, *Flowering Plants and Ferns of Arizona*, wrote:

"This plant has been a mainstay of existence to Southwest aborigines. When cultivated crops failed, they subsisted mainly on mesquite beans. Pinole, a meal made from the long sweet pods, prepared in the form of cakes and often as gruel, was a staple for the Pimas and still is eaten by them."

The beans were gathered in enormous quantities, ground up, pod and all, into a flour, which in turn was formed into cakes, dried in the sun, and stored in baskets.

There are at least eight uses for the mesquite bean and bark. The bean is one of nature's sugars, sweet enough to use for flavor in jelly, syrup, bread, and cookies. In the spring when the desert is at its best—fragrant, flowering, welcoming, and whispering with birds and small animals—picking mesquite beans can be an adventure. Grinding and pounding are another matter. I hand-ground mesquite beans for flour, and my work schedule totaled a half-hour of grinding for a half-cup of flour.

Poshol

The River People, the Pimas, were early farmers. Ruins in Pima territory trace corn back 1200 years and irrigation at least 1000 years. Yet the first Pima woman I came to know well said most of them carried or had water hauled to their homes on the Salt River Reservation near Scottsdale.

Eventually, many of them got modern homes with electricity and water. Still, they loved their traditional foods and kept outside stoves for cooking. Mrs. Catherine Pratt, an associate tribal judge, collected old recipes such as poshol, a kind of succotash, combining tepary beans and wheat rather than lima beans and corn—the succotash I knew.

Wash beans, wheat, and soup bone. Put in large pot and cover with boiling water. Cover and cook until beans are tender, about four hours on low, steady heat. Add salt the first hour. Serve with warm flour tortillas. Sometimes this was accompanied by "Indian spinach," greens growing wild which are dried. They lose color but not flavor, and cook up green and salty tasting.

| 2 cups white tepary beans |
| 2 cups whole wheat kernels |
| 1 large soup bone |
| salt to taste |

Papago Tepary Beans

Teparies, an arid-land crop apparently domesticated by prehistoric Indians, are tiny beans with five times more protein than the pinto. It was believed that one meal of teparies fueled the eater for a full day, whereas other beans had to be eaten twice. Because of this preference, the bean eaters were called the "Bean People."

Rain may not fall; bugs may invade the teparies. But these rugged little beans grow faithfully. The only place I ever have seen them for sale is at trading posts on the Tohono O'odham (Papago) Reservation. The little brown label gave directions for cooking beans "Bawi or Papago style." Put one cup of beans in a pot, add three cups of water and one tablespoon lard. When tender, add another tablespoon lard and one teaspoon salt, then continue cooking until thickened.

Further research indicated that when the Spanish found the Papagos eating this little bean, they asked its name. "It is a bean," which is *"t'pawl"* or *"t'pawi"* in Papago and became tepary to the invaders. They are a tasty little bean *if* soaked overnight, or twelve hours, before cooking. They double in size.

Tepary Soup

Papago is the language of the Desert People (Tohono O'odham), about 14,000 Indians living in scattered villages through Southern Arizona and Northern Sonora, Mexico. Recently the tribe voted to renounce the word Papago and assume Tohono O'odham as their official name. But the soup remains the same, perfect with fry bread, which they may call popovers.

Drain soaked beans and bring to boil with water in big pot. When they are tender, which will take longer than other beans, fry bacon until limp. Remove from pan. Add onion, carrots, celery, and garlic to bacon drippings. Sauté over low heat until celery is tender. Add bacon, then tomatoes and juice and spices. Cook 10 minutes. Add to beans. Cook another hour or until beans are mealy-tender.

Dried red chile pepper may be stirred into the pot the last 10 minutes, if desired. Serves 6 with flour tortillas or fresh fry bread.

2 cups tepary beans, soaked
6 cups water
4 slices bacon, diced
1 medium onion, chopped
2 carrots, sliced
1 cup celery, sliced
1 whole clove garlic, diced fine
3 cups tomatoes, with juice
1 teaspoon mixed oregano and cumin

Quelites

Quelites is a Spanish term for greens, a spring gift of the gods to be carefully hunted and picked. Some greens are so tender and tasty, they can be eaten raw when the first young plants tip-green the earth. Watercress, mint, miner's lettuce, lamb's quarter, and purslane all found a place in Arizona's heritage diet. Spring dandelion was almost a staple for the pioneers, who sliced and cooked the roots as a delicate vegetable, made a salad of the raw leaves, and boiled the bigger plants with salt pork or bacon.

"Wild greens are usually found after a spring rain. It is best to pick them when they are tender and before they flower," advised Nedra Lerma, from the Salt River Reservation. Her recipe seems to be basic for greens, whether from the desert, the mountains, or a small-town lawn.

Pick over greens, removing tough stems and brown leaves. Wash in several waters. Drain well. Dice bacon or salt pork and fry gently in heavy skillet until crisp but not too brown. Add onion and cook until clear. Remove bacon and keep warm. Add drained greens and stir into drippings until just thoroughly wilted. Sprinkle bacon or salt pork over greens and serve hot to 3 or 4.

4 cups quelites
1 onion, chopped
4 slices bacon, fried crisp, or chunk salt pork
¼ cup vinegar
¼ teaspoon salt

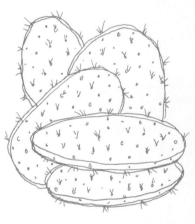

Nopalitos con Chile

Nopalitos can be found in the desert spring when the prickly pear cactus are putting on new shoots. The tender young pads are best to use, according to Fernanda Jiminez, who cooked at the Guadalupe Presbyterian School. Always pick with tongs or a folded newspaper.

With paring knife, scrape nopalitos on both flat sides, removing all spines. Cut shoots in small squares and wash well. In deep pan, boil until tender while chopping garlic and onion. Heat oil in separate pan and sauté onion and garlic 10 minutes. Drain nopalitos and save liquid. Combine flour, salt, pepper, and chile paste or powder with cooking broth, adding warm water if needed to make 1½ cups. Add to onion pan, returning to heat, stirring to medium-thin sauce. Cool 10 minutes. Add the tender cactus and cook 15 minutes on low. A different and piquant side dish to serve with beef, pork, or chicken.

12 cactus shoots, or nopalitos
2 cloves garlic, chopped
⅓ cup onion, chopped
¼ cup cooking oil
1 teaspoon salt
½ teaspoon pepper
2 tablespoons flour
2 ounces red chile paste or powdered chile
1½ cups warm water or broth

Table Mustard

Growing up, I became part of the spice and promise of late summer canning, peeling or chopping while the grown-ups bottled ketchup and jarred mustard pickle. Still, our families never made mustard. At a Coconino County Fair, a 4-H leader gave me this recipe for mustard from an old family cookbook. She said they used wild mustard, yellow flowers and all, in salad.

When the Padres were blazing a trail, legend has it they planted mustard seed along the way to make a conspicuous yellow trail for others—and for their return. Mustard greens are too bitter for many, but the thought of drying and grinding wild mustard seeds to cook into a condiment is a tasty challenge.

6 tablespoons ground mustard seed
4 tablespoons sugar
2 eggs
1½ cups apple cider vinegar
1 teaspoon butter
1 finely diced jalapeño pepper, seeded, optional

Mix mustard, sugar, and eggs in saucepan until smooth. Add vinegar and cook over medium heat, stirring constantly until mixture boils. Add butter, lower heat, and cook, bubbling gently, 5 minutes, stirring often. Thin with a bit more vinegar if needed. Cool and transfer into little pots or jars. For hot mustard, add the diced jalapeño pepper.

Creosote

My first intoxicating whiff of creosote was in the rain at the base of Camelback Mountain before any houses had usurped the desert. It was love at first scent, and I've tried to keep an angled branch in our house ever since because of the way it absorbs cooking odors. Each year, as the creosote disappears more and more rapidly, I grow increasingly grateful to the Indians who neighbor with it in peace.

Kay Betts, an Apache Junction desert herbalist and former columnist for *The Los Angeles Times Home Magazine*, traced the family tree of creosote bush for the *Herbarist*. Known also as horsebane, greasewood, and chaparral tea, creosote once dominated thirty million acres of Southwestern desert. According to Papago mythology, Itoy, their beloved deity, knew when the great flood was about to engulf the earth. Because his home was in the land of the creosote bush, he made a floating creosote-gum boat and bobbed safely around the world four times before landing intact back on Baboquivari Mountain.

Natives have long known of creosote's medicinal qualities. Smoked as medicine, swallowed as tea, steeped to become a poultice for man and beast, creosote was, and is, used as a soothing bath to relieve arthritis. The Spanish named it *gobernadora*, or the governess, because of its purported powers in regulating rheumatism and controlling infection, including venereal disease. *Falsa alca parra* was another Spanish name, meaning false caper bush in reference to its yellow buds—picked to eat as capers. It is high in digestible protein, yet I have never found a delicious creosote recipe. Its medicinal tea has more character than any other tea I've ever tasted.

Puffballs in Padding

The place to go in Arizona before biting into a wild mushroom became the Norman Sharber home in Flagstaff. He and wife Rayma Babbitt Sharber harvested meadow and forest food during 30 years of seasonal study. Rayma, who had earned her M. D. at Harvard, not only could identify an edible fungus jewel, she could pronounce it, dig it, cook, freeze, or dry it.

"There is no simple way to identify edibles. They are short-lived. Within a week, they'll come, blossom, and be too old, starting with the rains about the Fourth of July. With knowledge comes caution." Then comes the feast. "The giant puffballs, which have neither stems nor gills, grow at an elevation of at least ten to twelve thousand feet. They are wonderful, but so mild you can spoil them with overcooking." Not like this.

2 giant puffball mushrooms
3 beaten eggs
1 cup seasoned bread crumbs
½ cup French dressing
oil or butter

Slice puffballs fairly thick. Moisten with beaten egg. Dip in French dressing, then bread crumbs, and sauté in hot oil or butter until golden on both sides. Have at hand a crisp green salad and a bottle of wine. Feasts 4.

Apache May, who became devoted to John Slaughter after she was found as a tiny baby in an Apache camp in the Sierra Madres, nestles in a heap of pumpkins on Slaughter's San Bernardino Ranch. The child died tragically as the result of fire at the age of five or six, but loved her "Don Juan" to the end. ARIZONA HISTORICAL SOCIETY, TUCSON

Elderberry Cobbler

Emma and Roberta Baldwin grew up on a ranch in the Huachuca Mountains, near the border town of Sunnyside. They picked tiny, purple-blue elderberries from bushes growing in nearby washes, then ran home to wait impatiently for their mother to make jelly and cobbler. "Our cooking was on a wood stove. Before the days of commercial pectin, mother cooked apple peelings with the berries for natural pectin," Emma said. Her sister, now Roberta Lamma, wrote a book about those days, A Place Called Sunnyside. *The sisters still pick and can elderberries for the joy of a cobbler.*

Sift flour, baking powder, and salt. Work the butter into the flour with a fork or fingers. Add milk gradually until dough is soft and handles easily. Roll out on lightly floured board, using a floured rolling pin, shaping a round ½ inch thick to top a 10-inch cobbler or deep-dish pie plate. Mix elderberries, sugar, lemon juice, and cornstarch. Butter baking dish lightly. Pour in filling, top with crust. Slash to let steam escape. Bake 30 minutes at 375 degrees until top is golden, humpy brown. Extra good with chilled sweet cream, ice cream, or a little sour cream and nutmeg. Serves 6 to 8.

2 cups flour
4 teaspoons baking powder
scant cup milk or water
2 tablespoons butter
1 quart canned elderberries
2 cups sugar
4 tablespoons lemon juice
½ cup cornstarch
1 teaspoon salt
cream and nutmeg, optional

Marian's Palo Verde Peas

Marian De Grazia brought the desert into the dining room after she married Arizona's famed artist, Ted. "He taught me to eat things I never dreamed of tasting, like the new little pads of the prickly pear cactus. Slice and cook them plain before stickers emerge, with a little butter, not water. They have their own water. Best of all are palo verde peas. Catch them green on the tree before they dry. I eat them raw while I pick. Shuck them at once and freeze them in double plastic bags. Then take a handful out to use in many things. They are wonderful in an omelet. Moisture in the form of tomato or green chile adds just the touch needed to make them memorable as a vegetable side dish."

Sauté onion and garlic until clear in butter. Dice tomatoes into pan. Stir in green chiles and the soy sauce for salt and flavor. Blend, then add palo verde peas. Cook gently a few minutes and serve at once. Flavor and crunch pique the taste buds, the peas tender and green beyond any garden pea. Serves 2.

1 onion, chopped
1 clove garlic, chopped
1 scant tablespoon butter
2 fresh tomatoes, small
1 teaspoon green chiles, chopped
a few drops of soy sauce
1 cup palo verde peas, shucked

Squaberries

Arlene Naquayouma was born on the Gila River Indian Reservation in the Sacaton Hospital, "In the second building," she said, meaning the second hospital built there. She grew up living with Pima foods, then joined the staff of the Extension Service of the University of Arizona. She has seen interest grow in edibles from the desert. In native food workshops, she teaches as she cooks, using the unusual such as squaberries. The thorny bushes flower in early spring, growing along washes on dry desert slopes and beside farm fields. The red-to-orange berries ripen in May, rich in vitamins A and C. They may be eaten off the bush or dried in the sun like raisins. Arlene converts them to sauce or syrup.

Sauce: Combine berries, sugar, and water in heavy saucepan. Boil slowly until tender. Mash a few berries with spoon. Combine cornstarch and water. Stir slowly into berries. Mixture will thicken into a sunny sauce or pudding.

Syrup: Boil two cups fresh squaberries in 4 cups of water 1 hour, tightly covered. Strain, then reduce remaining liquid by boiling to a syrup. Use to make a healthy and refreshing drink by mixing the syrup with water and honey to taste. Or surprise the pancake crowd with a desert sunset syrup.

Sauce:

1 cup fresh squaberries
½ cup sugar or honey
½ cup water
2 tablespoons cornstarch
2 tablespoons cold water

Syrup:

2 cups fresh squaberries
4 cups of water

Agave Syrup

Viola Jimulla, deceased Chieftess of the Prescott Yavapai Indians, got up with the sunrise almost every day of her eighty-eight years. Her tribe lost 9.2 million acres in 1873 by federal decision and, by the time she became chieftess in 1940, the Prescott Yavapai occupied only seventy-five acres on the country's smallest reservation. Never bitter, always serene and humorous, Viola Jimulla became known as the tribe's outstanding basket weaver and historian. She brought the Presbyterian Church to Prescott.

Her fame as an excellent cook began when a student at Phoenix Indian School and was further enhanced as cook at the Blue Bell Mine near Mayer. She loved all kinds of food by her own admission. The only time we talked cooking, though, she spoke of old-time food gathering: prickly pears in June, saguaro fruit in July, acorns in August, and mescal in the fall. Mescal, or the century plant, is an agave best known for its baked heart. However, Viola valued the syrup made from agave leaves, admitting it was a lot of hard work. I never tried this recipe.

With a sharp stone or strong knife, chop the leaves from the mescal until there are enough to fill a cooking pot. Soak leaves, then cover with fresh water. Cook slowly several hours. Mash with wooden masher or stick. When pulpy, take off heat and cool enough to wring leaves into juice and pulp in the pot. Discard the leaves. Boil juice and pulp into a brown syrup, thick and sweet-smelling. Use to sweeten bread or mush.

Is it any wonder the Indians of long ago did not indulge in too many desserts?

Wild Grape Jelly

Wild grapes make delicious jelly. This is a 1920 recipe. It works fine, but keep the jelly in a cool, dry place.

Pick grapes over, wash well, and remove stems just before crushing into large heavy kettle. Add water and heat to the boiling point. Reduce heat to gentle rolling boil and cook until seeds are free. Press through jelly bag to strain, keeping count of number of cups of juice resulting. Return juice to kettle and bring to a boil, then add ⅔ cup sugar for each cup of juice. Boil quite rapidly, stirring with wooden spoon around sides of kettle, until juice jells. Skim and pour into sterilized glasses. Cover with melted paraffin.

Wild Grape Catsup: Thick, smooth fruit sauces were often used with meat instead of tomato catsup. A quart of wild grapes were cooked on low until soft for about half an hour, then put through sieve. The resulting grape puree was cooked with 1 cup of vinegar, a mix of spices (about 1 teaspoon each of cinnamon, cloves, ginger, dry mustard, and pepper), and a cup of sugar, if needed. Sugar and vinegar were adjusted according to family tastes. Bottle and seal and store in cool place.

Wild Grape Ratafia: Bruise grapes to make a pint of juice. Combine with 1 pint brandy and 10 ounces of sugar. Infuse for a fortnight, then strain and bottle.

Culinary Encyclopedia of 1832.

4 pounds wild grapes, crushed
1 pint water
sugar

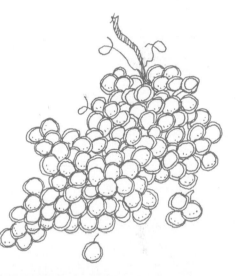

Wild Grapes

"The wild grape (*Ampelocissus acapulcensis*) grows in damp ravines, climbing over willow, poplar, and mesquite trees," recorded Juan Nentvig in 1764. "The fruit is quite acid and occasionally is used to make vinegar and even wine."

Much later, Canyon grapes were researched by Carolyn Niethammer in the same areas of the Southwest he traveled. She reported that some were eaten fresh and the remainder dried for use in flavoring other foods. Grape leaves, rather than wine, were used to allay thirst—by simply chewing a leaf or two.

A few years ago, some of the *Arizona Highways* staff went into Tonto Rim wild grape territory to produce material for a future issue. The hospitable Tonto Cowbelles entertained them, dishing up frijoles, jerky gravy on fresh, hot rolls, salad, and an Arizona-Texas Sheet Cake. Earlier, they boiled up some wild grape jelly and picked out black walnuts to send home to the wives so they wouldn't feel left out. The Old West lives for those lucky enough to go to the right places.

Glossary

Acorn - nut of the oak tree, an Apache cooking basic.
Agave - desert plant used for food, syrup, and drink.
Ajo - garlic.
Almendrado - almond pudding made in the colors of the Mexican flag: red, white, and green.
Alum - from the alum root, used to keep pickles crisp.
Andirons - iron braces used to hold logs and cooking utensils in fireplace.
Apothecary - druggist.
Arbuckles - most prized coffee of the Old West, roasted in sugar and egg white.
Arroz - rice.
Ash bread - Apache crusty bread baked in the coals of open fire.
Aspick - old term for clear gelatin mold boiled down from calves' feet; aspic.
Batter pudding - cooked custard, first boiled in a bag.
Bear sign - ranch term for doughnuts.
Biscochitos - Mexican sugar cookies.
Blade of mace - the inner section of nutmeg.
Blanc mange - flavored, thickened milk pudding.
Blue corn bread - Indian flat bread made with blue cornmeal.
Borracho - drunken (bo-rah-cho).
Brine to float an egg - water with enough salt to bear a raw egg; used for pickling vegetables and meat.
Browned flour - wheat flour browned in oven or fry pan, especially favored by Mexican and pioneer cooks for gravy and stew.
Buñuelos - fried fritters or cookies.
Burro - flour tortilla encasing a meat or bean filling.
Buttermilk - liquid left after butter is churned solid, prized as a drink or for cooking, flecked with butter bits.
Café - coffee.
Caldo - soup (Mexican).
Calf fries - ranch treat of quick-fried calf scrotum; also called mountain oysters.
Caliche - white crystal also known as saltpeter, soda niter, Chile caliche, and sodium nitrate.
Capirotada - Mexican bread pudding with cheese and spices.
Carne - meat.
Carne machaca - battered meat, seasoned with chiles and lime juice.
Carne seca - dried meat.
Castor sugar - old term for finely granulated sugar kept in a castor.
Charlotte - bread or cake pudding covered with fruit or gelatin.
Chayote - Mexican pear-shaped gourd cooked as squash.

Chile - at least sixty varieties of hot pods indigenous to Mexico; originally *"chilli"* from the Nahautl dialect of the Aztecs, adapted into Spanish as *"chile"* (spelled with an "e" rather than an "i"); *Capsicum frutescens.*
Chile caribe - dried red chiles, crushed, roasted, and simmered in water to liquid fire.
Chile colorado - chile con carne made with red chiles.
Chile con carne - a Mexican dish of meat with chiles.
Chiletepins - button chiles of gasp-inducing heat.
Chile verde - chile con carne made with green chiles.
Chili, chili con carne - an American colloquial term for thousands of versions of non-Mexican chile con carne; a bowl of red.
Chipotle - jalapeño smoke-dried for flavor.
Chorizo - spiced Mexican sausage, popular with eggs and potatoes.
Chuck wagon - kitchen on wheels used on the range.
Cider - juice from pressed apples used as a drink or as vinegar.
Cilantro - Mexican parsley; a spice used fresh or dried; coriander.
Clabber - thicken to curds and whey; sour cream.
Cobbler - deep-dish fruit dessert baked with rich pastry topping or biscuit dough.
Cochineal - small red bug crushed to make red coloring.
Coffee mill - hand mill for grinding coffee beans.
Comal - Mexican griddle.
Comfit - fruit or root (as ginger) dried and preserved with sugar.
Comino - cumin, seasoning signature of Mexican food, especially in salsas.
Con queso - (kohn keh-soh) with cheese.
Conserve - jam of mixed fruits, usually with nutmeats.
Cooler cabinet - box of tin shelves covered with heavy material to wet down for food storage.
Coriander - the seed can be traced to the Old Testament: "And the manna was as coriander seed." The plant is an herb also known as cilantro, the popular Mexican parsley, expecially noted in fresh salsas.
Corn cakes - small cakes made from cornmeal; fried mush slices served with syrup or honey.
Corn pone - fried corn cakes.
Cracklings - crisp, chewy residue left when lard is rendered.
Cream - to mix butter or other fat with hands or forks until soft and fluffy, usually with sugar.
Creamed vegetables - thickened with white sauce; also eggs, fish, and meats; popular until being lean became more popular.
Creosote - desert plant used as medicine and for tea.

---

*T*he Bashford House sits as an elegant reminder of a different era. Built in the 1870s, the residence was only about a year old when it was acquired by William C. Bashford and his wife, the former Mary Louise Evans. The home they bought for $2,000 was a rectangular, two-story, frame structure. They immediately set about enlarging and remodeling it. Besides the "gingerbread" trim that characterizes many homes of its period, the Bashford House has other design characteristics that make it a worthy example of Victorian style.

At one point in its life, the Bashford House appeared destined for demolition. In 1974 the site, on Prescott's main thoroughfare, was to be developed for a fast-food restaurant. But the house itself was given to the Prescott Historical Society. In a flurry of civic activity, fund-raising events were put together and $25,000 was raised to move the house to its present site.

Restored in its original style, Bashford House now hosts special events and is open to the public as part of the heritage exhibit at Sharlot Hall Museum.

Table settings from the museum collection recreate a Bashford tea party.

Cruda - raw.

Cumin - distinctively aromatic, the seeds are used whole in Mexican dishes and curries; used ground in Mexican dishes and sauces; cumino.

Cumino - Spanish word for the aromatic cumin flavoring.

Cure - preserve by salt and/or spices.

Cut and fold - spoon down through a mixture, then bring to the top, folding over lightly as spooned upward.

Dash - one shake; ⅛ teaspoon.

Dessert spoon - scant teaspoon.

Dogie - cowboy term for cow.

Dripping - meat fats cooked out during frying or broiling, most often used to flavor other dishes.

Dulce - sweet.

Dutch oven - heavy cast iron pan, usually three-legged, with a thick lid removed by center handle.

Empañadas - Mexican filled pastries.

Enchiladas - filled corn tortillas with cheese topping.

Escabeche - pickled.

Fajitas - meat strips braised with onions, chiles, and spices.

Fermented - activated by yeast.

Field peas - black-eyed peas.

Fines herbes - mixture of finely crushed herbs.

Flan - Mexican custard of milk, cream, or canned milk.

Fluff-duff - fancy grub like cakes or puddings; ranch term.

Fricassee - meat or chicken served in a rich milk sauce.

Frijoles - beans, usually pinto beans, from the Spanish.

Frito - fried.

Fritter - fruit, meat, or fish dipped in batter, then deep fried in hot fat.

Fry bread - see squaw bread or popovers.

Game - wild bird or animal.

Gazpacho - cold chopped vegetable soup.

Gem irons - iron muffin pans.

Giblets - liver, heart, and gizzard of poultry, sometimes fried, usually simmered until tender, then chopped to add to gravy.

Gill - ½ cup.

Gonch - hook used to lift lids from Dutch ovens.

Graham flour - whole wheat flour with the bran intact.

Green corn - fresh corn off the ear (cob).

Greens - any green leafy vegetable or edible weed.

Grits - ground hominy.

Grunt - ranch term for dough pudding.

Grunt and cluck - ham and eggs, in cowboy talk.

Guacamole - mashed, seasoned pulp of avocado.

Hangtown fry - fried oysters, gold rush style.

Hardtack - a hard biscuit or bread of flour and water only.

Haunch - hind quarters; hams.

Hazelnuts - filberts.

Hock - a joint in the hind leg.

Hoe cake - corn cakes cooked on a hoe.

Hominy - whole or ground hulled corn processed in a lye bath to remove the germ and plump the kernel; the Indian way is to cook the dried kernel with ashes.

Hops - the dried cones of the female flowers of the hop plant used in baking, beverages, or medicine.

Indian meal - yellow cornmeal.

Indian pudding - cornmeal and molasses pudding, steamed in husks by early Indians.

Irish moss - a moss used as thickener.

Isinglass - gelatin made from fish viscera.

Jalapeño - (hal-a-pain-yo) fiery hot, small, green pepper.

Jam - preserve from whole fruit boiled to a pulp with sugar.

Javelina - desert wild pig.

Jelly bag - small muslin bag used to hold fruit during jelly making.

Jerky - dried meat in strips, highly seasoned.

Junket - a sweet dessert made from flavored milk and rennet.

Kahlua - midnight-dark Mexican coffee liqueur.

Keg - small cask with a capacity of 5-10 gallons.

Kettle - a lidded pot for boiling and stewing.

Knead - to work dough on a flat surface, pressing or punching down with knuckles, then folding over and over.

Kneeldown bread - Navajo, fresh, corn-kernel bread baked in cornhusks in hot ashes; put in from kneeling position.

Lard - white, solid, rendered fat of a hog, the most-used shortening for the frontier cook.

Larder - cupboard where meat and other foods were kept.

Lardoons - strips of fat for larding meat, inserted in lean meats to add flavor.

Leaven - yeast or cream of tartar used as ingredient for doughs and batters to induce fermentation.

Lightnin' bread - quick breads leavened with saleratus, soda, or baking powder.

Lime water - calcium oxide.

Maize - corn.

Mano - smooth stone used to grind corn or seeds on the metate.

Marjoram - annual plant with aormatic leaves used for cooking.

Marrow - bone substance and gut enjoyed by Indians and pioneers.

Masa - corn dough for tortillas and tamales painstakingly made by hand-grinding corn on a metate with a mano.

Masa Harina - instant corn flour, a latter-day product developed by the Quaker Oats Company at the request of the Mexican government.

Menudo - fiery Mexican "hangover cure" soup made with tripe.

Mesquite - southwestern desert weed; used as fuel, it flavors foods uniquely; the beans are an Indian staple.

Metate - thick grinding stone with low side walls.

Mock turtle soup - calf's head, brains removed, cooked whole as soup meat.

Molcajete - grinding stone of volcanic origin.

Mole - sauce or paste of chiles, spices, and chocolate.

Mortar - hand receptacle for crushing or grinding with a pestle.

Mother - slippery small mass of yeast and bacteria to be added to wine or cider to make vinegar.

Mull - to heat and spice a beverage.

Mush - cornmeal boiled thick.

Mutton - edible meat of a fully grown sheep, especially favored for stew by Hopis and Navajos.

Nanakopsie - Hopi spring green.

Nixtamal - hominy.

Nopales - young pads of prickly pear cactus, edible and used fresh and cooked with chiles, vegetables, or eggs; sugared for candy.

Opuntia - prickly pear cactus.

Orange water - drink or seasoning liquid distilled from orange peels.

Oregano - mint family plant used for seasoning.

Orehones - dried fruits.

Ox - large, strong cattle with tail used for soup.

Pad - stems or leaves of prickly pear used in cooking.

Pan - bread.

Panadería - bakery.

Panocha - Mexican brown sugar.

Papago - "Bean People" of South Central Arizona who subsisted basically on mesquite and tepary beans; the Tohono O'odham Nation.

Parch - to dry; to cook in dry heat until almost scorched.

Paste - suet dough.

Pavo - Spanish for turkey; also el guajalote or el turque.

Pectin - fruit or vegetable gelatin.

Pemmican - of Indian origin; dried, pounded meat mixed with fat and berries, pressed in cakes for survival food, later adapted by the U.S. Army.

Piki - Hopi, blue-corn, batter bread baked as thin and crisp as paper.

Pima - "River People" who lived on the banks of the Gila River.

Pinole - a food-drink of parched, ground cornmeal and water.

Pinto bean - Arizona favorite, speckled like the horse.

Plants - the four sacred plants of the Southwest Indians are corn, beans, squash, and tobacco.

Pooch - cowboy favorite of stewed tomatoes, sugar, and biscuits.

Popover - Indian fry bread; also a quick muffin made without leavening, which necessitated hand beating.

Pothook - bent iron for hanging a pot or kettle over the fire.

Pound cake - true pound cake has a pound each of butter, eggs, and sugar.

Pudding cloth - bag or cloth in which to boil pudding.

Purslane - desert greens.

Put down - put food into cellar, wooden boxes, or larder for storage; to cure pork or corn beef.

Quelites - wild spring greens.

Quick bread - also known as lightnin' bread, popular after baking soda and baking powder were formulated.

Quick lime - unslaked lime.

Quick oven - hot; 450 to 500 degrees.

Rajas de chile - strips of chile.

Range - a wood or coal stove; the wide open spaces of the West.

Rat cheese - store cheese used in early recipes and as rat bait.

Relleno - stuffed.

Render - to cook meat until fat liquefies and can be strained.

Rennet - made painstakingly from the fourth stomach of calves; used in cheese production or junket pudding.

Ristra - string of dried chiles.

Rounded spoonful - heaped.

Rub in - mixing flour or cornmeal and fat or suet with fingers.

Saddle blankets - cowboy name for big pancakes.

Saguaro - desert plant which grows to 50 feet, may live over 200 years; furnishes fruit as a staple to desert Indians.

Salamander - various articles used with fire, from stove to utensil.

Saleratus - early, coarse-grained baking soda.

Salsa - sauce, especially Mexican hot sauce.

Salt hoss - cowboy term for corned beef.

Saltpeter - nitre; used to preserve meat.

Salt rising - without yeast, moist but crumbly bread.

Saltspoon - ⅛ teaspoon.

Sausage casing - entrails cleaned to be stuffed with sausage.

Scrapple - meat dish of freshly butchered pork scraps and cornmeal.

Scrolls - Serbian fried bows of brandied dough.

Shortening - fat of many kinds, butter and lard to drippings.

Short'nin' bread - sweet, rich-quick bread.

Sippets - small piece, usually of toast, soaked in milk or broth for the sick; bits of toast or biscuit for garnish.

Skillet - was a small, three-legged kettle; now a fry pan.

Slap bread - hand-shaped bread, slapped thin, as tortillas, fry bread.

Sopa - soup, dry or liquid.

Sopapillas - small fried pillows of bread.

Sourdough - yeasty fermented bread, a camp cook favorite kept in a keg or crock.

Spotted pup - chuck wagon name for raisin pudding.

Squab - young, plump pigeon.

Squaberries - red-orange berries from thorny desert bushes.

Squaw bread - Indian bread deep-fried in six-inch circles, also known as fry bread and popovers.

Suet - firm fat of cows and sheep used to cook and make tallow.

Sweetbreads - thymus glands from very young veal and beef.

Taco - word means "wad" or "mouthful"; crisp shell with meat filling.

Tallow - firm fat of animal.

Tallow biscuits - hot biscuit spread with fresh tallow.

Teacup - ½ cup, old measure.

Tomatillos - small green vegetable, distinctive flavor, looks like little tomato.

Tostada - Historically, flour tortilla fried flat, crisp; later covered with cheese, beans, and other combinations.

Treacle - English word for dark molasses.

Tripe - comes from the first and second stomach of a cow (oxen).

Tub - half-barrel.

Tuna - fruit of prickly pear cactus.

Turnovers - pastry circle filled with fruit or meat, turned over in halves.

Vanilla bean - The seed pod of an orchid which becomes flavoring extract when soaked with grain alcohol and water; from the Spanish *vainilla*, "little sheath."

Veal - meat from calf no older than eight weeks.

Venison - past term for any bird or animal dressed as game; now, deer meat.

Verdolagas - common southwest green; purslane.

Voul-au-vent - puff pastry to be filled with fruit or meat.

Wash - brushed with egg white.

Waterglass - sodium silicate used as preservative for eggs.

Whey - watery liquid remaining after curds are taken from milk.

Yucca - desert plant used for soap, weaving baskets, and food; the banana-like fruit is roasted.

Zest - citrus peel, scraped to use as flavoring.

Mary Riordan hosts a tea party for her small friends at what today is Riordan State Historic Park.
COURTESY ARIZONA STATE PARKS

Index

Acknowledgments

The writer extends warm and grateful thanks to the Arizona State Museum and the First Families; Arizona Historical Society and Heather Hatch and Susan Leubbermann; the Special Collection staffs at Arizona's Universities; Sharlot Hall Museum and the Ruffner family; the Marguerite Noble Library and the Payson Historical Society; Stella Hughes; Betty Accomazzo and all the Arizona Cowbelles; Florence Historical Society; the women of the University of Arizona's Extension Services, and Ellen Cooke's cooks and their creative cookbooks from churches and schools and community groups all over the state.

Also, thanks are due to staff members at Heritage Square Foundation, Pipe Spring National Monument, Hubbell Trading Post National Historic Site, the Fort Huachuca Museum, Pioneer Arizona, Yuma County Historical Society, Tucson Museum of Art, and to Belinda Nelson of the Gila Indian Center, Dr. Reba N. Wells of the Arizona Historical Society, Robert W. Munson of Riordan State Historic Park, Johnson Historic Museum of the Southwest which operates John Slaughter's San Bernardino Ranch, Kemper Bales of the Bill Williams Mountain Men, Carol Augustin who, with her husband, both restored and researched the history of the Hawes Home, and Phyllis Allen, Pat Small, Alva Torres, Marcia Hartwell, and John Walsh.

Famous for its gardens and its aviary, the E.F. Sanguinetti home in Yuma was a perfect setting for the family's festive parties. The Century House now is headquarters in Yuma for the Arizona Historical Society.
ARIZONA HISTORICAL SOCIETY YUMA